# THE AMAZING PENNSYLVANIA CANALS

## 150th
## Anniversary
## Edition

By
WILLIAM H. SHANK, P.E.

First Printing, First Edition, July 1960
Second Printing, Second Edition, December 1965
Third Printing, Third Edition, October 1973
Fourth Printing, Third Edition, January 1975
Fifth Printing, Third Edition, October 1977
Sixth Printing, Anniversary Edition, June 1981
Seventh Printing, Anniversary Edition, September 1986

Published By
AMERICAN CANAL AND TRANSPORTATION CENTER
809 Rathton Road, York, Pennsylvania 17403

ISBN 0-933788-37-1

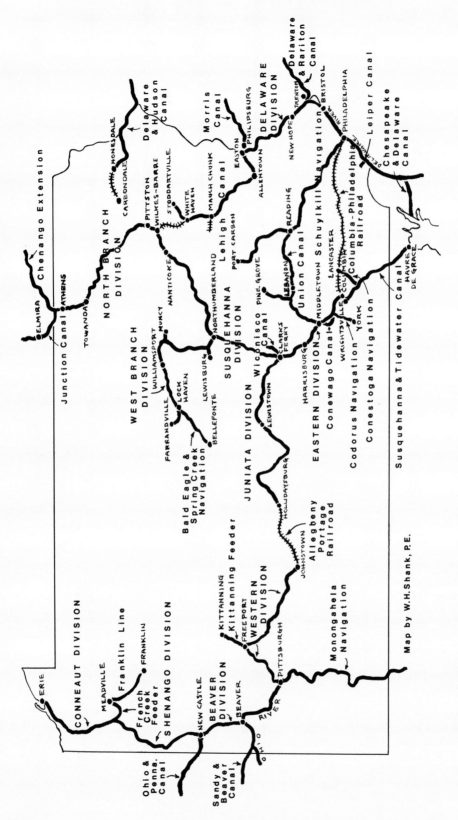

This map shows all the 1243 miles of state-owned, or privately owned canals operated within the boundaries of Pennsylvania over a period of nearly 135 years. Not all of these canals were in operation concurrently. Also indicated are the state-owned or privately owned railroads which formed an integral part of the canal system. Connecting canals or navigation systems to the six surrounding states are also shown. (Map prepared by the author)

# CONTENTS

Pre-canal transportation in Pennsylvania was by Flat-Boat or "Ark" floating downstream, usually on a spring "freshet".

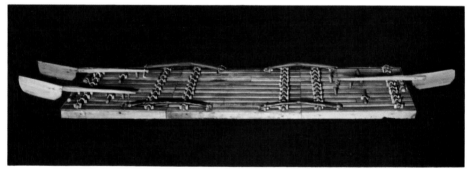

A hewed Timber Raft of the type that once crowded the Susquehanna and Allegheny Rivers. (Model by H. B. Rhines, Carnegie Museum.)

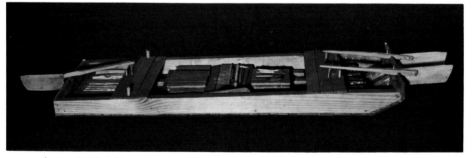

A rough Flat-Boat for the river trade — a favorite of the western emigrants. (Model by H. B. Rhines, Carnegie Museum.)

# INTRODUCTION

During the year 1831, the Western Division of the Pennsylvania "Main Line" opened to traffic between Johnstown and Pittsburgh; the Susquehanna Division Canal was completed between Clarks Ferry and Northumberland; and the North Branch Canal, between Northumberland and Nanticoke began operation. The following year — 1832 — the Delaware Canal, from Easton to Bristol and the Juniata Division of the "Main Line" between Amity Hall and Hollidaysburg both opened for business. In 1834 the Columbia-Philadelphia and Allegheny Portage Railroads began operation, as part of the "Main Line" Canal System between Philadelphia and Pittsburgh.

A few, privately-owned canals were already in operation, but the year 1831 saw the real beginning of the State-operated network of canals in Pennsylvania which were to bear the major passenger and freight traffic load in the Keystone State for the next several decades. Hence, the year 1981 becomes the 150th Anniversary Year for the active start of tow-path canals for transportation in Pennsylvania. For this reason, I have named this book "The 150th Anniversary Edition" of THE AMAZING PENNSYLVANIA CANALS.

This Edition contains much material not found in previous editions, including canal data tables never gathered in one publication previously. It also contains many illustrations, transferred from the PENNSYLVANIA MAIN LINE CANAL by McCullough and Leuba, last published by the American Canal and Transportation Center in 1976, and now out of print. We are indebted to Authors McCullough and Leuba for the use of their tables. We have expanded considerably on these tables with the help of canal buffs throughout the State, as listed in the Acknowledgments section. We hope that our combined efforts have resulted in a fairly comprehensive, working guide-book to the historic Pennsylvania Canals, while not neglecting the nostalgia and romance of those long-gone days in our State's history.

William H. Shank, P.E.

York, Pennsylvania

June, 1981

Packet boat entering a lock on an eastern canal.

## THE CANAL BOOM OF THE EARLY 1800's

From the days of the early settlement of the American east coast the need for better avenues of travel westward was evident, as our restless forefathers moved further and further inland. William Penn, for instance, 100 years before the Revolutionary War, envisioned a canal connecting the Schuylkill River with the Susquehanna to provide water travel from Philadelphia to the wilderness of western Pennsylvania. George Washington, while still a young surveyor, made many exploratory trips over the foot trails of the Alleghenies to lay plans for avenues of travel to the northwest, which later culminated in the "National Road" running west through Maryland and across southwest Pennsylvania to the Ohio River, and still later in the Chesapeake and Ohio Canal, running west from Washington into the Allegheny Mountains.

After our forefathers had made the great break with their mother country, they became a struggling young nation stretched along the Atlantic sea coast from the district of Maine to the state of Georgia with an inland potential which many of the pioneers of the day were already reporting to be rich in natural resources. This inland area could only be reached commercially by the long voyage down the Atlantic coast, around Florida, up the Mississippi (whose lower extremities were still controlled by the French), and up the Ohio. The Allegheny Mountains stood as a formidable barrier to western commerce across Pennsylvania, Maryland and Virginia. Even if the British had not controlled the St. Lawrence there was no direct water connection from the eastern seaboard to the Great Lakes. The steam locomotive had not yet been invented, hence railroads, as we know them, were unheard of.

The National Road, a hard-surfaced highway originally proposed by George Washington and completed in 1820 from Baltimore to Wheeling, West Virginia, was one of the first relatively successful efforts to pierce the Allegheny Mountain barrier to the West.

In Pennsylvania in the early 1800's the Philadelphia-Lancaster Turnpike afforded relatively good transportation between these two cities. A connection west from central Pennsylvania was made by wagon trails known as Forbes Road and Kittaning Path. With the increase in travel some of these roads were widened but their condition west of Harrisburg was not otherwise much improved. One writer, in 1812, stated: "It requires a good team of five or six horses from 18 to 35 days to transport 2500 to 3500 pounds of goods from Philadelphia to Pittsburgh."

In England, the use of canals as a means of commercial transportation had been developed with great vigor in the last several decades of the 1700's. After the Revolutionary War Robert Fulton, a native of Lancaster County, later to become famous as the inventor of one of the first successful steamboats, had spent considerable time in England studying the canal systems of that country. He had developed a number of inventions for their improvement, few of which proved to be of practical value. However, Fulton was in communication with George Washington, president of the new United States, as well as with John F. Mifflin, governor of Pennsylvania, around 1796, promoting the use of small canals in his native state, as well as throughout the new country generally. Fulton's contacts with Washington may have influenced the latter to push through plans which ultimately resulted in the Chesapeake and Ohio Canal, and also to take a lively interest in the development of the Union Canal in Pennsylvania.

The canal "boom" in the United States really began in New England around 1800 and spread gradually westward as New York, Maryland, Pennsylvania, Virginia and the Carolinas all started investigating means of transportation to the new northwestern territories of Indiana, Kentucky and Illinois by means of man-made waterways or improvements, con

The famous Union Canal Tunnel just west of Lebanon. 729 feet in length, it was cut through solid rock using hand pick and shovel and crude blasting methods. It pierced the watershed ridge on the summit level of the Union Canal between Reading and Middletown. Boats were poled through the tunnel, while the mules climbed over the hill.

necting or supplementing existing streams and rivers.

The first really significant canal project west of the New England states took shape in 1810 when plans were laid by the state of New York for the building of a canal from Albany on the Hudson to Lake Ontario. These plans were interrupted by the War of 1812 and when the project was actually commenced in 1817, the influence of possible future hostilities to the North led to a change of plans. The canal route was altered to go directly west to Lake Erie at Buffalo, completely by-passing Lake Ontario and the barrier of Niagara Falls, thus opening the western Great Lakes to the Atlantic Coast by way of New York City and the Hudson River. The "Erie Canal," as it was soon named, was completed in 1825 and proved an extremely bold and farsighted move on the part of New York State. It was largely responsible for the rapid growth of the modest port of New York City into one of the world's greatest seaports.

# UNION AND SCHUYLKILL CANALS

The State of Pennsylvania, while slow to get into the canal building business, at least had the distinction of having one of the oldest canal systems in the country. In 1797 the Conewago Canal, paralleling the Susquehanna River on its west bank below York Haven and designed to enable boats to avoid the rocks and rapids of Conewago Falls, had been built and declared operable by the state. Its purpose was to link south-bound river traffic safely with Columbia, to make connection with the Philadelphia-Lancaster Turnpike. (Years later, 1818 to 1840, the Hopkins Canal performed a similar function on the east bank of the Susquehanna at Conewago Falls.)

Further, the Union Canal, which ultimately connected the Schuylkill River at Reading with the Susquehanna River at Middletown, had the distinction of being the first canal route ever to be surveyed in America. The approximate route for the Union Canal was first conceived by William Penn. Having laid out Philadelphia in 1682, which became the country's first great seaport, Penn issued proposals for another city in the province of Pennsylvania in 1690 as follows:

"It is now my purpose to make another settlement upon the river Susquehanagh . . . and the most convenient place for communications with former plantations in the east . . . which will not be hard to do by water by benefit of the river Scoulkill, for a branch of that river (Tulpehocken Creek) lies near a branch that runs in the Susquehanagh River (Swatara Creek) and is the common course of the Indians with their skins and furrs into our parts . . . from the west and northwest parts of the continent."

A picnic boat out-bound from Lebanon on the Union Canal, around 1870.

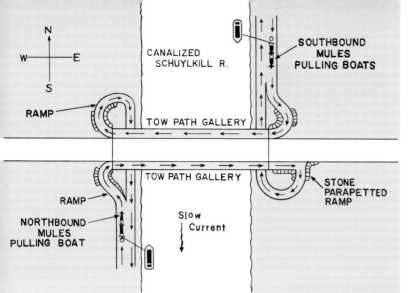

N · W—E · S

CANALIZED
SCHUYLKILL R.

SOUTHBOUND
MULES
PULLING BOATS

RAMP

TOW PATH GALLERY

TOW PATH GALLERY

RAMP

STONE
PARAPETTED
RAMP

NORTHBOUND
MULES
PULLING BOAT

Slow
Current

Towpath pattern at Stoudt's Ferry Bridge near Reading showing the method of transferring the towpath from one side of the river to the other, without unhitching the mules. ( Courtesy George R. Wills )

Schuylkill Navigatic at Port Clinton abo 1885. ( Courtesy Heydinger )

This canal connection was discussed for many years, and in 1762 David Rittenhouse, the astronomer, and Dr. William Smith, provost of the University of Pennsylvania, made surveys over Penn's route from Reading to Middletown, the route later traversed by the Union Canal.

The Revolutionary War intervened before anything further was done. In 1792 two companies were chartered by the State of Pennsylvania to build a navigable waterway between the Schuylkill and Susquehanna, improve the Schuylkill from Norristown to Reading, and build a canal from the Delaware River to Norristown. By 1794, the companies had completed 15 miles of work, including several locks, and had spent $440,000, which exhausted their funds, and the work ground to a stop— for the next twenty-seven years. The legislature granted the companies the right to raise another $400,000 by means of lotteries, but by 1811 the two companies, united under the name "Union Canal Company," had managed to raise only $60,000.

In 1815 by act of the Pennsylvania legislature a new enterprise, the "Schuylkill Navigation Company," was chartered to complete the work on the Schuylkill River. The portion of the Schuylkill which was made navigable extended from Port Carbon, just above Pottsville, to Philadelphia, a distance of 108 miles. Of this route, 62 miles were by canal, and 46 miles by so-called "slack water navigation pools" in the river itself, formed by a series of dams passed in each case by locks. Between Port Carbon and Philadelphia there were 92 lift locks to overcome a 588-foot difference in elevation. Locks on the Schuylkill Navigation system were 80 feet long by 17 feet wide. Much of the trade using the system consisted of arks, rafts and boats carrying anthracite from the coal region into Philadelphia.

An interesting side note on the construction of the Schuylkill system was a 450-foot-long tunnel, completed in 1821 near Auburn, Pennsylvania, through which the canal passed. The tunnel was constructed through a low hill, which might easily have been avoided by laying out the canal line about a hundred feet westward. However, the proprietors of the company wanted a tunnel, knowing that it would be the first one to be constructed in the United States. The tunnel grew to be a great curiosity and people came from as far as Philadelphia to see it. It was shortened from time to time until about the year 1857, when it was reduced to an open cutting. The Schuylkill Navigation Company continued to operate from 1825 until 1870 when it was sold to the Philadelphia and Reading Railroad Company, one of its largest customers. Under the new management the system continued operations until 1931.

In the meantime the Union Canal Company, whose responsibility had now been narrowed to the water route between Reading and Middletown, was offered financial aid by the state of Pennsylvania due to the impending threat to Pennsylvania's commerce of New York State's partially completed Erie Canal. With this additional impetus the Union Canal was pushed through to completion between 1821 and 1828, to make a water link between Philadelphia and the Susquehanna.

The Union Canal, 4 feet deep, 36 feet wide at surface level and 24 feet wide at bottom, was a remarkable feat of engineering. In a distance of 81 miles (by canal) between Reading and Middletown it climbed 311 feet to the summit level of the canal at Lebanon and descended a total of 192 feet to the level of the Susquehanna River at the west end, using a total of 93 lift locks 75 feet long and 8½ feet wide.

The summit level was approached by a consecutive series of 19 locks on the west side and 7 consecutive locks on the east side of Lebanon.

In addition, just west of Lebanon the canal ran through a 729 foot tunnel in the water shed ridge. Completed in 1826, it was the second tunnel in the country, and is today maintained by the Lebanon County Historical Society as the "oldest tunnel in the United States."

An additional 22-mile feeder, making connection west of Lebanon brought water from a large reservoir, created north of Blue Mountain, to supply the summit level of the Union Canal. (The Pine Grove Feeder.)

The Union Canal, costing a total of $6,000,000, was traversed in the spring of 1828 by its first boat, the "Fair Trader," which finished the trip from Philadelphia to Middletown in five days.

Maintaining water in the summit level of the Union Canal was a tremendous problem. The limestone soil allowed rapid water leakage, which was subsequently offset somewhat by lining the canal walls with heavy planks at the bottom and sides. Inasmuch as the feeder canal was located some 85 feet below the summit level it was necessary to pump the water from the feeder canal junction (known as the "Water Works") using four huge pumping engines, rated at 120 H.P. apiece and two immense water wheels 40 feet high by 10 feet wide, to raise the water through a 3-foot-diameter wood pipe to the top of a 95-foot hill from which point the water flowed four miles through an aqueduct to the summit level of the canal.

Unfortunately the designers of the Union Canal had been too conservative and had made both the channel and the locks of the canal so narrow that the heavy freight boats and large passenger packet boats, which soon made their appearance on most of the eastern inland waterways, could not use the canal. Special boats able to carry a load of only 25 to 28 tons were constructed for the Union Canal. The canal proprietors secured permission from the state legislature to widen their channel in 1841 but the enlargement was not actually completed until 1856. After spending an additional $6,000,000 for this enlarging program the Union Canal was then able to handle boats of from 75 to 80 tons capacity, but the company never recovered from this enormous additional expenditure, and it was finally abandoned in 1885.

The original narrow design of the Union Canal thus prevented it from assuming anything more than a secondary role in the Philadelphia-Pittsburgh canal system.

# THE "MAIN LINE" CANAL SYSTEM

"Penn Lock" on the Main Line Canal at Harrisburg, about 1890. The canal ran through downtown Harrisburg just east of the present Amtrack Railroad Station.

The building of the New York state's Erie Canal, which began in earnest in 1817; plus a petition of the Delaware and Hudson Canal Company (incorporated in New York in 1823) asking for permission to extend its lines into Pennsylvania; not to mention Maryland's National Road, completed in 1818 from Baltimore to the Ohio River, all made it increasingly and painfully evident to the citizens of Pennsylvania that they had little means of east-west cross-state transportation to tie the two ends of their state together commercially. In the 1700's Philadelphia was the leading seaport on the Atlantic Coast, but by 1820 it was obvious that with the aggressive steps being taken by both neighboring states of New York and Maryland the ports of New York City and Baltimore would rapidly outstrip Philadelphia, unless the latter improved its means of communication to the new western territories.

The citizens of Pittsburgh were particularly outspoken in their appeal to the Pennsylvania state legislature for some transportation medium which would link them with the seaboard. Although railroads were now being talked of, a canal system was generally favored, particularly since the Union Canal Company was finally making progress in its efforts to tie the Schuylkill and Susquehanna Rivers together.

Tandem freight boats headed upstream in the lock at Dauphin. The lower gates have been closed and the lock tender is preparing to open the upper "drop type" gate after the water level rises in the lock.

Thus, with public pressure rapidly increasing, the state legislature of Pennsylvania successively passed three canal acts. The first was dated March 27, 1824 and instructed Governor J. Andrew Shulze to appoint three commissioners whose duties should be to examine a canal route to lead "from the great valley of Chester and Lancaster Counties along one or another set of natural waterways westward to Pittsburgh."

The second act, dated April 11, 1825 was to consider and adopt measures directed toward the establishment and implementation of "navigable communication between the eastern and western waters of the state and Lake Erie." Five commissioners were now designated to investigate not less than seven different waterways across the state.

The third act (February 25, 1826) authorized "the commencement of a canal, to be constructed at the expense of the state and to be styled "The Pennsylvania Canal." This act empowered the commissioners to begin construction immediately of canals at three points: First, along the Susquehanna River from Swatara Creek to the Juniata River; second, along the Allegheny River from Pittsburgh to the Kiskiminetas River; and third, down French Creek to connect by feeder with Conneaut Lake.

Ground was broken by Governor John Andrew Shulze for what was later to be known as the "Main Line Canal" at Harrisburg July 4, 1826 with much ceremony.

Chickie's Lock on the Eastern Division Canal, two miles north of the Columbia basin, circa 1890. A pair of tandem boats are shown rising to the next level.

Lock at Steelton circa 1895. Water is today maintained in this section for industrial use.

The Eastern Division Canal followed the east bank of the Susquehanna. Here it passes under the Pennsylvania Railroad bridge at Rockville.

Waste-way on the Eastern Division near Dauphin, with triple sluice gates to allow surplus water to return to the river.

# The Eastern Division

The Eastern Division of the Pennsylvania Canal, while the first section to be started, was the last of the three Main Line canal divisions to be completed. Originally this section was to connect with the Union Canal at Middletown and then run north, along the eastern bank of the Susquehanna, for 24 miles to Duncan's Island at the mouth of the Juniata River. However, the plans were changed in 1828 when the commissioners were authorized to extend the eastern division of the canal to a new terminus at Columbia, Pennsylvania, 19 miles further south, from which point a railroad connection with Philadelphia was contemplated. Thus the Eastern Division ultimately ran 43 miles from Columbia to Duncan's Island, with a total of 14 locks, including an outlet lock to permit access from the canal basin at Columbia to the Susquehanna River. The locks were constructed of cut stone masonry and were for the most part 90 feet in length by 17 feet wide, with an average lift of approximately 7½ feet.

The Eastern Division generally followed what was known as a "contour" route, skirting the base of the hills and winding as close to the river as possible to maintain a level grade. The "fill" excavated in cutting into the river bank to produce the canal channel was thrown to the river side to produce the tow path.

At points where the canal had to cross other streams entering the river a water bridge, known as an "aqueduct" carried the canal channel across. At the mouth of the Swatara Creek at Middletown, for instance,

Columbia Canal Basin about 1896 looking southwest from a hill north of Columbia. The outlet lock to the river is clearly visible at the center of the photograph. (Courtesy Clinton H. Pressler)

Lock on the Main Line Canal north of Columbia, using "drop type" gate at the upper end. Chickie's Rock in the background.

a 300 foot long aqueduct with a water channel 18 feet wide and 4 feet deep, carried the canal across the creek at this point, with a road bridge attached at one side.

When the Eastern Division Canal reached the junction of the Susquehanna and the Juniata 15 miles above Harrisburg, the engineers ran up against their first major problem. They had to get the canal across to the west bank of the Susquehanna to pick up the entrance to the Juniata Division Canal and also to make connection with the newly authorized branch running up the west bank of the river, known as the Susquehanna Division. It was decided to build a dam between the lower end of Duncan's Island and the east bank of the Susquehanna, at Peter's Mountain, to form a deep and more or less placid pool across which canal boats could be drawn from a towing path bridge. Hence a dam 1998 feet long and 8½ feet high with a base 30 feet thick was built of strong timbers with an embankment of broken stone and gravel. A short distance above the dam the canal commissioners then built the first Clark's Ferry bridge, a covered wooden structure with a double-deck tow path down-stream. The pool formed by the dam also provided water for the entire Eastern Division of the canal.

Two additional liftlocks on Duncan's Island (first two locks on the Susquehanna Division) raised the boats from Clark's Ferry pool to a junction with the Juniata Division on Duncan's Island at a canal basin just south of the old Amity Hall Inn. The Eastern Division was put into operation early in 1833.

# The Western Division

The Western Division Canal was authorized to start at Pittsburgh and run upstream along the Allegheny River from Pittsburgh to a junction with the Kiskiminetas River at Freeport.

The same legislative act of February 25, 1826 which had started work on the Eastern Division empowered the commissioners to proceed immediately with construction east from Pittsburgh. However, work did not get underway quite as promptly at this end of the state because there was considerable debate about the selection of a suitable route. Surveys were run on both banks of the Allegheny. The citizens of Pittsburgh favored a south bank route, which would bring the canal into the heart of old Pittsburgh, but the terrain on that side of the river made a north bank route much more feasible. Citizens of the newly incorporated borough of Allegheny on the north side of the river directly opposite Pittsburgh were delighted at the prospect of a canal terminal in their community. They argued that the freight and the passengers could be drayed across the Allegheny River into Pittsburgh at little additional

Second canal aqueduct at Pittsburgh. The first was an all wooden covered bridge structure. This one, built in 1845 by John A. Roebling, designer of the Brooklyn Bridge, was the first cable suspension bridge in the country.

cost. However, Pittsburghers objected vehemently. They indicated that they had not agitated all these years for a canal, to have it terminate in a neighboring borough. A compromise was finally effected in the form of an aqueduct across the Allegheny River, entering Pittsburgh opposite the Grant-Liberty junction. This aqueduct was the longest and most troublesome on the entire Pennsylvania Main Line route. A contract for the aqueduct was let on June 3, 1827, and when completed the structure was 1140 feet long, 14 feet wide at the bottom, 16½ feet wide at the top and 8½ feet deep with a foot bridge on one side, and tow path on the other. Heavy white pine planks 2½ inches thick, laid diagonally in two courses would, it was hoped, hold the great weight of water.

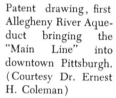

Patent drawing, first Allegheny River Aqueduct bringing the "Main Line" into downtown Pittsburgh. (Courtesy Dr. Ernest H. Coleman)

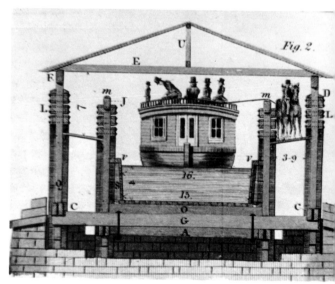

Another point upon which Pittsburghers insisted was that the canal should be run south through Pittsburgh to connect with the Monongahela River at a point where the proposed Chesapeake and Ohio Canal was supposed to enter the city. This proved to be a most expensive and difficult engineering feat since a 810-foot canal tunnel had to be constructed under Grant's Hill and a series of four additional lift locks had to be built through the heart of the city to lower the canal to the Mononga-hela River level. The main canal basin and unloading point for the terminus of the canal, however, was located on the north side of Pitts-

West portal of the 817-foot canal tunnel at Tunnelton, leading directly into the Conemaugh River Aqueduct.

burgh. The "turning basin" ran east and west between Penn and Liberty Avenues, and the canal terminal depot was located on the east corner of Grant and Seventh.

The borough of Allegheny finally won the right to have its own branch and separate terminal facilities on the north side of the Allegheny River with a series of four additional locks below the north end of the aqueduct, which permitted the canal boats to pass on down into the Allegheny River on that side. This connection proved quite valuable on the several occasions when the aqueduct collapsed.

After the foregoing details were settled, construction of the Western Division Canal proceeded along the northwest bank of the Allegheny to Freeport. Subsequently a 14-mile extension, known as the Kittanning Feeder, was built north along the Allegheny, terminating at Kittanning.

In 1827 the legislature authorized an additional 44 mile extension of the canal from the mouth of the Kiskiminetas up that stream and its major tributary, the Conemaugh River, as far as Blairsville. The following year a further extension was approved along the Conemaugh to Johnstown.

East portal of the Main Line Canal tunnel at Tunnelton. The dam to create slack-water navigation is shown at the right.

21

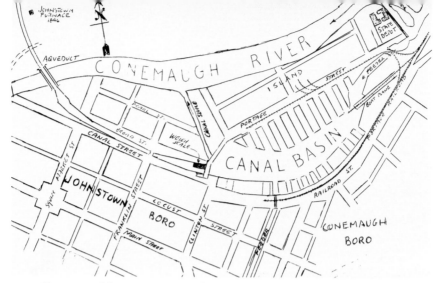

Downtown Johnstown in 1850, showing canal basin and Portage Railroad.

Construction on the Western Division followed the same pattern as the Eastern Division, with the canal channel measuring 40 feet at the top water line and 28 feet at the bottom, 4 feet minimum in depth. The locks, constructed of masonry as in the eastern division, were 90 feet long but only 15 feet wide. The total length of this section was 105 miles. Including the four lift locks between the Pittsburgh basin and the Monongahela River and the outlet locks in Allegheny Borough there were a total of 68 guard and lift locks.

There were also two canal tunnels on the route, one in downtown Pittsburgh as previously described, and the second along the Conemaugh east of Tunnelton. The latter, completed in 1830, was the third tunnel constructed in the United States. It was 817 feet in length and was built to avoid following the Conemaugh River on a long meandering loop. Exit from the west end of the tunnel was directly onto an aqueduct crossing the river.

Additional features of the Western Division were a total of 16 aqueducts, 10 river dams, 64 culverts, 39 waste weirs and 152 road bridges passing over the canal channel.

Newspaper accounts in the Pittsburgh area indicate that some traffic began to move on the Western Division by autumn of 1830 but it was not until May of 1831 that the first fully loaded freight boat from Johnstown arrived safely in Pittsburgh, with 7927 pounds of merchandise.

The Pittsburgh canal extension through Grant's Hill tunnel to the Monongahela River was not made operable until August of 1832. The Chesapeake and Ohio Canal never came closer to Pittsburgh than Cumberland, Maryland, so this extension and tunnel served mainly as a spillway to carry off excess water from the canal basin.

"Containerized" shipment is not new. The same idea was applied in loading canal "Box Boats" at Johnstown 130 years ago.

Exterior photo of the 412' aqueduct crossing the Conemaugh River from the west tunnel portal. (Courtesy Richard Steinmetz.)

Interior of the Western Division, 817'-long tunnel at Tunnelton, Pa. looking out over the west-portal aqueduct.

Dam and Lock Number Four on the Juniata Division near North's Island. The Millerstown Rope Ferry can be seen at the upper left.

# The Juniata Division

The Juniata Division of the Main Line Canal System began officially at the canal basin on the northwest corner of the triangle of ground where the Susquehanna and Juniata Rivers join, known as Duncan's Island. This old canal basin is still quite visible about 300 or 400 yards south of the Amity Hall Inn. Well preserved ruins of the No. 1 lift lock on the Juniata Division can still be found about 100 yards due west of this canal basin. Here the boats were elevated approximately 10 feet to the level of the 600-foot long Juniata aqueduct where the Main Line crossed the Juniata River. This wooden trough type aqueduct, with tow path on one side and a passenger path on the other, rested on five sturdy stone piers, three of which (as of this writing) are still standing, although the structure of the bridge has long since disappeared.

Eastern entrance to the No. 1 aqueduct on the Juniata Division near Amity Hall, about 1890. At this point the Main Line crossed the Juniata River.

Interior of the No. 1 aqueduct on the Juniata Division. Note towpath at left, wood-lined water channel, center, and pedestrian walk at right.

Artist's conception of the Hollidaysburg terminus of the Juniata Division, showing the Portage Railroad in the upper left background. (Courtesy Commercial Museum)

The Pennsylvania legislature authorized the first leg of the Juniata Division to be constructed in 1827. This was a 40-mile section, running from Duncan's Island to Lewistown, but before work on the line was much more than started subsequent acts of the legislature authorized an extension to Huntington and finally to Hollidaysburg, 127 miles up the Juniata from the Duncan's Island basin.

At North's Island, eighteen miles up the Juniata, the narrow water gap through Tuscarora Mountain made it necessary to swing the canal back to the north bank of the river. An eight-foot dam was constructed across the river at this point to provide a slack water pool across which the canal boats could be towed. An endless rope type ferry was employed for this purpose and the higher water level of the canal on the north side was used to actuate a water wheel, which worked the machinery for the ferry.

The dimensions of the canal channel cross section on the Juniata Division were the same as on other portions of the Main Line. The standard lock on the Juniata was 90 feet long by 15 feet wide—two feet narrower than those on the Eastern Division. In general the locks on this division were not as well constructed as on the Eastern and Western Divisions; four were of solid cut-stone masonry; seven were of so-called rubble stone laid in mortar, and the remaining 75 locks on the division consisted of wooden frames, planked water tight with boards 4 inches

26

Middle lock (of three) still standing in 1954 at Lockport, Mifflin County.

Lockport Lock, 1954. Some of the vertical timbers, which held the lock plank lining in position, are still evident.

The double-lift lock at Millerstown Rope Ferry, 1954. North side of the Juniata River. (Photo by Walter Leuba)

Millerstown lock-tender's house as it appeared in 1954. (Photo by Walter Leuba.)

28

thick, the sides being supported by walls of dry masonry with heavy puddling (a mixture of mud and clay) worked in at the ends to keep the water from escaping through the fill. Each lock had a flume or spillway along the inland side four feet wide and two feet deep with shut-off gates to regulate the water permitted to pass the locks.

From North's Island the canal ran along the north bank of the Juniata as far as Huntingdon, with three dams across the river at various points to feed water into it.

Above Huntingdon it was found necessary to build 14 river dams to provide pools for the 16 miles of slack-water navigation on that part of the line. The canal followed its own channel in this section for only 22 miles of the route. The balance of the navigation was in the river itself, with the tow path alternating from one bank to the other, whichever side proved more expedient.

The Juniata Division required 86 locks to overcome a change in elevation of 584 feet in the 127 miles between Duncan's Island and Hollidaysburg. There were 25 aqueducts to carry the canal over the larger tributaries, mainly wooden structures on stone piers.

It had originally been planned to end the Juniata Division at Frankstown, but due to the resistance of a farmer who owned the land at the

Juniata Division of the Main Line at Millerstown. At this point the canal crossed the Juniata River via a water-driven rope ferry, shown at the upper right. A double lock was used to overcome the change of level at this point.

point where the canal basin was originally planned, the canal was extended two miles further west to Hollidaysburg.

Extension of the terminus of the canal brought with it some additional problems in supplying the summit level of the canal with sufficient water. Reservoirs were ultimately constructed at three different points on various tributaries of the Juniata above Hollidaysburg to keep the upper reach of the canal full of water.

The Juniata Division was officially opened to traffic with the passage of the packet boat "John Blair" between Huntingdon and Hollidaysburg on November 27, 1832. It was subsequently discovered that some of the workmanship along that section was faulty and certain locks and several of the aqueducts had to be rebuilt before full operation was possible the following year.

## The Allegheny Portage Railroad

From the days of the early planning of the Main Line, the plan for passing Allegheny Mountain had been somewhat nebulous. The original surveys indicated that there would be no great difficulty following the routes of the Susquehanna, Juniata, Conemaugh, Kiskiminetas and Allegheny Rivers with a canal, but the one big obstacle on this route had, from the first, been Allegheny Mountain between Hollidaysburg and Johnstown.

One plan originally considered was the running of the canal approach south of Hollidaysburg along a small tributary of the Juniata, virtually to the base of Allegheny Mountain, and a similar extension east of Johnstown along a tributary of the Conemaugh, which would have brought the ends of the Juniata and Western Divisions within approximately six miles of each other. A four mile canal tunnel through Allegheny Mountain was suggested as the final connecting link.

So anxious were the citizens of Pennsylvania and the legislature at Harrisburg to get something started that the canal bills authorizing the initial construction on the eastern and western divisions were rushed through before any serious thought was given to the tunnel.

As construction of the Main Line system moved rapidly up the waterways approaching Allegheny Mountain from both east and west, the canal commissioners realized that they had a much greater problem on their hands than they had anticipated.

First of all the idea of a four-mile tunnel through Allegheny Mountain had the engineers of the day shaking their heads dubiously. At that time

Canal boat sections ascending Plane #6 of the Allegheny Portage Railroad, highest of five inclined planes on the Hollidaysburg side of Allegheny Mountain. The cable cars were operated by stationary steam engines at the top of each plane. (Courtesy Commercial Museum)

Lemon House, an inn and passenger station on the summit line of the Allegheny Portage Railroad, 2397 feet above sea-level. The power house for Plane No. 6 is in the background. (Courtesy Commercial Museum)

Looking east down Plane #6 on the Allegheny Portage Railroad. The bridge in the background is the famous "Skew Arch," still standing, where the Huntingdon, Cambria and Indiana Turnpike crossed the Portage. (Courtesy Dr. Ernest H. Coleman)

the only other tunnels in the United States were on the Schuylkill Navigation system, the Union Canal, and the Main Line itself. None of these tunnels measured more than 850 feet in length. Even today the digging of a four-mile tunnel would be a major undertaking. The prospect of such an enterprise in 1828 was overwhelming.

Even if the tunnel had been completed, its elevation would have been at such a height that the maintenance of proper water level in this section of the canal would have presented tremendous problems. Already difficulties were being encountered in obtaining sufficient water supplies for the upper reaches of the Juniata and Western divisions. As previously mentioned, large reservoirs were being created above Hollidaysburg for the Juniata division, and the famous Johnstown Dam was being constructed to supply water to the Conemaugh section of the Western Division.

The canal commissioners reluctantly abandoned the Allegheny Tunnel and turned their attention to another means of passing the mountain. A turnpike was considered, but due to the extreme steepness of the grade on the east side of the mountain the canal commissioners finally decided upon a Portage Railroad.

Thus came into being one of the most unusual means of overland transportation ever devised, before or since. The Allegheny Portage Railroad was authorized by an act of the Pennsylvania legislature and approved by the Governor on March 31, 1831. The line was surveyed and located by engineers working under the direction of the Canal

Commissioners, who on May 25, 1831 let the contract for that part of the road between Johnstown and the summit of the mountain. Contracts for the work between the summit and Hollidaysburg were awarded on July 29 of the same year. The first track was completed on March 18, 1834. The route was open for traffic at that time and the second track was completed late in the spring of 1835.

Basically, this 37-mile railroad consisted of a series of ten inclined planes, five on one side of the mountain and five on the opposite side. Traffic, of course, moved both upward and downward on both series of planes. Each plane had two tracks with an endless hemp cable moving up one track and down the other, to which the ascending or descending cars were attached. An attempt was usually made to balance the weight of the ascending cars against the descending cars at each plane. When the ascending weight was greater than the descending weight, stationary steam engines at the head of each plane were used to supply additional power. When the descending weight was greater, an ingenious water-cylinder brake was used to control the speed of descent. In between the planes were stretches of track with a slight up-hill slope over which the cars were initially transported by horse or mule power, later by primitive steam locomotives. The planes were numbered from the Johnstown end of the route and varied in length from 1500 feet (plane No. 3) to 3100 feet (plane No. 8). The slope of the planes varied from a minimum of 6% (6 foot rise to 100 feet) on plane No. 9 to a maximum of 10% on

Conemaugh viaduct on the Allegheny Portage Railroad, east of Johnstown, which was destroyed during the Johnstown flood. (Courtesy Dr. Ernest H. Coleman)

Plane #8 on the Allegheny Portage Railroad, about five miles west of Hollidaysburg. The loading area may be seen at the lower right. (Courtesy Jesse L. Hartman)

plane No. 7. The highest point on the route was at the top of plane No. 6 on the Hollidaysburg side, 2397 feet above sea level, nearly 1400 feet above the level of the canal basin at Hollidaysburg and approximately 1170 feet above the Johnstown station at the west end of the route. The horizontal tracks were laid on two rows of stone "sleepers" with metal fasteners set into the rock. The tracks of the planes were iron straps nailed on wooden rails and held in place by wooden cross-ties.

Travel along the Portage Railroad can perhaps be best described by means of excerpts from the writings of some of its passengers. One such literary traveler was a Philadelphia writer who used the pen name "Peregrin Prolix." This gentleman, whose real name was Philip Holbrook Nicklin, traveled the route from Johnstown to Hollidaysburg August 20, 1835. Here is his description of the trip over the Portage Railroad:

"Yesterday at Johnstown we soon dispatched a good breakfast and at 6 AM were in motion on the first level, as it is called, of four miles length, leading to the foot of the first inclined plane. The level has an ascent of 101 feet and we passed over it in horse-drawn cars with a speed of six miles an hour. This is a very interesting part of the route, not only on account of the wildness and beauty of the scenery, but also because of the excitement mingled with vague apprehension which takes possession of everybody in approaching the great wonder of the internal improvements of Pennsylvania. In six hours the cars and passengers were to be raised 1172 feet of perpendicular height and be lowered 1400 feet of perpendicular descent by complicated, powerful and frangible machinery, and were to pass a mountain, to overcome which with a similar weight three years ago would have required the space of three days. As soon as we arrived at the foot of Plane No. 1 the horses were unhitched and the cars were fastened to a rope which passes up the middle of one track and down the middle of the other. The stationary steam engine at the head of the plane was started and the cars moved

34

majestically up the steep and long acclivity in four minutes, the length of the plane being 1608 feet, with perpendicular height of 150 feet.

"The cars were now attached to horses and drawn through a magnificent tunnel 900 feet long having two tracks and being cut through solid rock nearly the whole distance. (This was the first railroad tunnel built in America.) Now the train of cars were attached to a steam tug (locomotive) to pass a level of fourteen miles in length. This lengthy level is one of the most interesting portions of the Portage Railroad from the beauty of its location and the ingenuity of its construction. It descends almost imperceptably through its whole course, overcoming a perpendicular height of 190 feet. The valley of the Little Conemaugh is passed on a viaduct of the most beautiful construction. It is of one arch, a perfect semi-circle with a diameter of 80 feet.

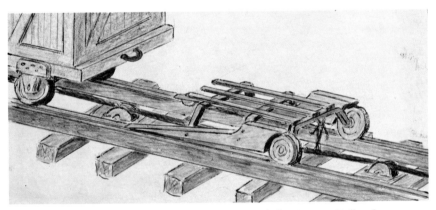

Safety car used on the inclined planes of the Portage Railroad.

"The fourteen miles of this second level are passed in one hour and the train arrived at the foot of the second plane, which has 1760 feet of length and 132 feet of perpendicular height. The third level has a length of one and five-eighths miles, a rise of 14½ feet and is passed by means of horses. The third plane has a length of 1480 feet and a perpendicular height of 130 feet. The fourth level is two miles long, rises 19 feet, and is passed by means of horses. The fourth plane has a length of 2196 feet and a perpendicular height of 188 feet. The fifth level is three miles long, rises 26 feet, and is passed by means of horses. The fifth plane has a length of 2629 feet and a perpendicular height of 202 feet and brings you to the top of the mountain, 2397 feet above the level of the ocean, 1172 feet above Johnstown and 1399 feet above Hollidaysburg.

"Thus three short hours have brought you from the torrid plain to a refreshing and invigorating climate. The ascending apprehension has left you but it is succeeded by the fear of the steep descent which lies before you and as the car rolls along on this giddy height the thought trembled in your mind that it may slip over the head of the first descending plane, rush down the frightful steep and be dashed into a thousand pieces.

"The length of the road on the summit of the mountain is one and five-eighths miles and about the middle of it stands a spacious and handsome stone tavern. The eastern quarter of a mile, which is the highest part of the entire route is a dead level; in the other part there is an ascent of 19 feet. The descent on the eastern side of the mountain is much more fearful than the ascent on the west for the planes are much longer and steeper, of which you are made aware by the increased thickness of the ropes, and you look down instead of up.

"There are also five planes on the eastern side of the mountain and five slightly descending levels, the last of which is nearly four miles long and leads to the basin at Hollidaysburg. This is traveled by cars, without steam or horse, merely by the force of gravity.

"In descending the mountain you meet several fine prospects and arrive at Hollidaysburg between 12 and 1 o'clock.'

The figures quoted by Mr. Nicklins are not necessarily the same as those preserved by the Pennsylvania Railroad in its files of statistics on the Portage Railroad. However, they are reasonably close.

A famous English author who traveled the Allegheny Portage Railroad in 1842 was Charles Dickens. Here is his account of the crossing of Allegheny Mountain on his way from Harrisburg to Pittsburgh over the Main Line of the Public Works:

"On Sunday morning we arrived at the foot of the mountain, which is crossed by railroad. There are ten inclined planes; five ascending and five descending; the carriages are dragged up the former and let slowly down the latter by means of stationary engines; the comparatively level spaces between being traversed sometimes by horse and sometimes by engine power as the case demands. Occasionally the rails are laid upon the extreme verge of a giddy precipice and looking from the carriage window, the traveler gazes sheer down without a stone or scrap of fence between into the mountain depths below. The journey is very carefully made however, only two carriages traveling together and while proper precautions are taken, it is not to be dreaded for its dangers.

"It was pretty traveling thus at a rapid pace along the heights of the mountains and with a keen wind, to look down into a valley full of light and softness catching glimpses through the treetops of scattered cabins;

"Hitching up" a sectional canal boat train at the foot of Plane Number Eight on the Portage Railroad.

Interior view of the Allegheny Portage 900-foot tunnel, oldest railroad tunnel in the United States. (Photo courtesy Earl B. Giles.)

A train of sectional canal boats on the Allegheny Portage Railroad crossing the Ebensburg Branch Viaduct near Wilmore.

One of the high-level "giddy precipices" described by Charles Dickens during his trip over the Allegheny Portage Railroad.

Portage Railroad tunnel, 900 feet long, the first railroad tunnel built in America. Motive power in the tunnel was horses.

children running to the door; dogs bursting out to bark, whom we could see without hearing; terrified pigs scampering homeward; families sitting out in their gardens; cows gazing upward with stupid indifference; men in their shirt sleeves, looking on at their unfinished houses, planning out tomorrow's work; and we riding onward high above them like a whirlwind.

"It was amusing too when we had dined and rattled down a steep pass, having no other moving power than the weight of the carriages themselves, to see the engine, released long after us come buzzing down alone, like a great insect, its back of green and gold so shining in the sun that if it had spread a pair of wings and soared away no one would have had occasion, as I fancied, for the least surprise. But it stopped short of us in a very business-like manner when we reached the canal; and before we left the wharf, went panting up the hill again with the passengers who had waited our arrival for the means of traversing the road by which we had come."

Many European travelers took the Main Line route in preference to the Erie Canal or other routes across to the western states simply because of the reputation which the Allegheny Portage Railroad had acquired as one of the most spectacular routes to be enjoyed by the traveler in North America.

39

Eastern terminus of the Philadelphia and Columbia Railroad at Stock Exchange corner in Philadelphia, about 1843. A sectional packet boat is leaving, via rail for Columbia.

## Columbia and Philadelphia Railroad

In few sections of the state through which the Pennsylvania system of public works passed is the expression "Main Line" today more than just a memory. At the Philadelphia end, however, the term "Main Line" has stuck, and is used in referring to the various suburbs strung along the Lincoln Highway, immediately west of Philadelphia, although most of the inhabitants have forgotten the origin of the expression.

The state-owned Columbia and Philadelphia Railroad, extending 82 miles from Vine and Broad Streets in Philadelphia to the canal basin at Columbia, was started in 1828 and completed in 1834—one of the earliest railroads in America and the first in the world to be built by a government rather than private enterprise.

As previously mentioned, the Union Canal might have formed the eastern link in the Main Line from Philadelphia to Pittsburgh and did ultimately take some of the traffic between Philadelphia and the Susquehanna River. However there was considerable pressure upon the Canal Commissioners by the citizens of Chester and Lancaster Counties for a more direct route to the Susquehanna, through their areas.

In 1827 the Canal Board was authorized to make surveys and estimates for both canal and railroad routes between Philadelphia and the Susquehanna, through Chester and Lancaster Counties. It was quickly decided that a railroad would be more feasible, because the hilly country made a canal route difficult and expensive.

At the time of the decision to build the Columbia-Philadelphia Railroad no really satisfactory steam locomotive had yet been invented, so the railroad was planned with horses as the motive power. The line was designed with two inclined planes, one at each end. On the east end was the Belmont Plane, 2805' long with a lift of 187', located on the west bank of the Schuylkill River several miles north of central Philadelphia. From Broad and Vine Streets the railroad followed the abandoned right of way of the defunct Delaware and Schuylkill Canal, to the Schuylkill River which was crossed, at the foot of the Belmont Plane, by means of a 984' viaduct.

The plane at the west end was located in Columbia, to lower the cars to the level of the canal basin. It was 1800' long and 90' high. Both planes were operated by stationary steam engines at the top, in the same fashion as the inclined planes of the Portage Railroad. The stretch of railroad between the Belmont and Columbia planes was relatively low-grade, and was ultimately double-tracked the full length of the line.

The Columbia and Philadelphia Railroad was officially opened by Gov. George Wolf April 15th, 1834. Steam locomotives had now been developed in England. Hence the first train over the line (in which the governor's party rode) was powered by an English-built locomotive known as the "Black Hawk." This train made the first run between Columbia and Philadelphia in two days, including a number of stops for ceremonies and celebrations along the line.

The railroad was at first considered a public thoroughfare, with the State's interest being limited merely to the collection of tolls. Anyone

Belmont Inclined Plane, looking east, with the Schuylkill River in the background. The "Columbia Bridge" shown here was still in use for local wagon traffic close to the turn of the century.

with a vehicle which would fit the track and had the means of propelling it (either horse or steam power) was permitted to use the line as long as he paid the proper toll. Particularly during the first six-month period, when only one track was available, the resulting confusion, brawling and ill will which resulted were completely indescribable.

The State realized that it would have to exercise some sort of scheduling and control over the entire line and finally bought its own locomotives and ran them at regular intervals to haul cars owned by individual shippers. They also attempted to separate the locomotive drawn traffic from horse drawn traffic on the road by publishing, on March 28, 1836, a ruling that all locomotives must leave the Belmont plane between 4 and 10 in the morning and between 5 and 8 in the evening. The last one out in each period was to carry a special signal to let everyone know that it was safe to start out with horse-drawn cars. Even with this separation of traffic by motive power there were many delays because of the absence of sidings to permit the fast trains to pass the slower ones moving in the same direction.

The earliest locomotives were wood burners, but anthracite coal was successfully introduced in 1838. The following year, bituminous coal from the western end of the state was tried and was found even better than anthracite. Horses were banned from the line entirely April 1st of 1844, when the state elected to provide motive power for all cars being moved between the Belmont plane and Columbia. The addition of a telegraph line along the right of way in 1850 considerably improved the efficiency of the entire operation.

For a description of travel on this interesting, early railroad, we turn again to the works of writer Philip Nicklin of Philadelphia. Nicklin writes of his trip from Philadelphia to Columbia August 1, 1835:

"We sat down to breakfast at half past seven, and were just in medias res, compounding in a large wine glass that 'nauseous mixture' composed of a little chloride of sodium, or muriate of soda, or common salt, and a soft boiled fresh egg, when the anticipated Omnibus drove to the door, a bad half hour earlier than the agent had promised, causing us to swallow our coffee, furious hot, with haste. As there was no remedy, leaving a longing, lingering look behind at the rescued half of our breakfast, we stowed ourselves and baggage as quickly as possible.

"We proceeded to the Depot in Broad Street to be transferred to a Rail Road Car. After a quarter of an hour of confusion, the passengers and their trunks being at length segregated, the former were packed

State-owned Philadelphia and Columbia Railroad passing through Lancaster, 1842.

inside and the latter outside. We had chosen a unilocular car of oval shape with a seat running round the entire inside, so that the nose of each passenger inclined towards some point in a straight line drawn between the two foci of the ellipse.

"Two cars filled with passengers and covered with baggage are drawn by four fine horses for about four miles to the foot of the inclined plane, which is on the western bank of the Schuylkill and is approached by the spacious viaduct extending across the river, built of strong timber and covered with a roof. The cars had scarcely begun to move when it was discovered that they were on the wrong track in consequence of the switchmaster having left the switches open, and everybody wished them applied to his own back. This error being rectified by a retrograde movement, at length the cars started on the right track at the rate of six miles an hour.

"The ride to the foot of the plane is very interesting, first passing through a deep cut made forty years ago for a canal that was never finished, and then by a number of beautiful islands in the foreground, and the banks on both sides occasionally rising into bold hills crowned with romantic villas.

"At the foot of the inclined plane the horses were loosed from the cars; several of which (the number being in inverse proportion of the

43

weight) were tied to an endless rope, moved by a steam engine placed at the top of the plane, and presently began to mount the acclivity. When the cars had all arrived at the top of the plane, some twelve or fourteen were strung together, like beads, and fastened to the latter end of a steam tug, which was already wheezing, puffing, and smoking, as if anxious to be off. All these little ceremonies consumed much time, and the train did not leave the top of the inclined plane until ten o'clock.

"The inclined plane is more than nine hundred yards in length and has a perpendicular rise of about one hundred and seventy feet; it occasions much delay and should be dispensed with, if possible.

"After many stoppings to let out passengers and let in water, and after taking into our eyes many enchanting views and millions of little pestilent triangular cinders, we arrived at Lancaster at 3 P.M. without accident or adventure.

"The Columbia Rail Road is made of the best materials, and has cost the state a great sum; but it has some great faults. The curves are too numerous, and their radii generally too short, in consequence of which the journey to Columbia (eighty miles) consumes seven or eight hours, instead of four or five. The viaducts are built of wood instead of stone, and the engineer, doubting their ability to bear the weight of two trains at once, has brought the two tracks on them so close together as to prevent two trains passing at the same time. Accidents have occurred from the collision of cars upon these insufficient viaducts. Their roofs are so low as to prevent the locomotives from having chimneys of a sufficient height to keep the cinders out of the eyes of the passengers and to prevent the sparks from setting fire to the cars and baggage. The chimneys of the steam-tugs are jointed, and in passing a viaduct the upper part is turned down, which allows the smoke to rush out at so small a height as to envelop the whole train in a dense and noisome cloud of smoke and cinders.

"Notwithstanding these inconveniences, a fine day and a beautiful country made our day's ride very pleasant; as we soon found that the smoky ordeals could be passed without damage by shutting our mouths and eyes and holding our noses and tongues.

"We took up our quarters for the night at Mrs. Hubley's Hotel in Lancaster and found the accommodations very comfortable.

"We left Lancaster at 5 A.M. next morning in a railroad car drawn by two horses, tandem; arrived at Columbia in an hour and a half, and stopped at Mr. Donley's Red Lion Hotel where we breakfasted and dined, and found the house comfortable and well kept.

Terminus of the Pennsylvania State Railroad at Columbia, about 1842. At this point the sectional boats were lowered into the canal basin to start their water journey to Pittsburgh. (Courtesy Pennsylvania Railroad Company)

"Columbia is twelve miles from Lancaster, and situated on the eastern bank of the noble river Susquehanna; it is a thriving and pretty town, and is rapidly increasing in business, population, and wealth. There is an immense bridge over the Susquehanna, the superstructure of which, composed of massy timber, rests upon stone piers. This bridge is new, having been built within three years.

"Here is the western termination of the Rail Road, and goods from the seaboard intended for the great west are here transshipped into canal boats.

"At 4 P.M. we went on board the canal boat of the Pioneer Line to ascent the canal, which follows the eastern bank of the Susquehanna."

## Main Line "Portable Boats"

In October of 1834 an event occurred on the Allegheny Portage Railroad which in some degree changed the mode of travel across the entire Main Line system. The incident was recorded in a local publication as follows: "In October of this year the Portage Railroad was actually the means of connecting the waters of western Pennsylvania with those of the Mississippi. Jesse Chrisman, from the Lackawanna, a tributary of the north branch of the Susquehanna, loaded his boat 'Hit or Miss' with his wife, children, beds and family accommodations, with pigeons and other livestock and started for Illinois. At Hollidaysburg, where he expected to sell his boat, it was suggested by John

45

Dougherty, of the Reliance Transportation Line, that the whole outfit could be safely hoisted over the mountain and set afloat again in the canal at Johnstown. Mr. Dougherty prepared a railroad car calculated to bear the novel burden. The boat was taken from its proper element· and placed on wheels where, under the superintendence of Major C. Williams, the boat and cargo at noon of the same day began their progress over the rugged Allegheny. All this was done without disturbing the family arrangements of cooking, sleeping, etc. They rested at night on the top of the mountain, like Noah's Ark on Ararat, descended next morning into the valley of the Mississippi and sailed for St. Louis."

This event led to the development of sectional canal boats, which could be drawn over the Portage Railroad in pieces, each section being completely water-tight in itself. When assembled in the water at either end of the Portage it became a complete canal boat. They were built in three or four sections. Here is a description of a four-section boat by Captain H. A. Walters of Lewistown, Pa., who started as a driver on the Pennsylvania canal in 1849:

"The sectional boats were 82 feet in length, 13 feet in width and in depth 12 feet, and were divided into four sections each 20½ feet long. The boats were round on the bottom. The sections were fastened together by irons about half way down the side—the iron projected out from the one section into a V-shaped iron on the other section, then a T-iron fitted down to both of these irons and locked them together. One section was placed upon one railroad truck which was a bit longer than the section—about 23 to 24 feet—and had four wheels. The trucks were round in the bottom to fit the boat sections."

We feel that Captain Walter's statement of the *width* of the boats is erroneous, as in order to pass on the various railroads the sections could not have been in excess of about 7'9".

In any event, a patent was granted to John Dougherty of Hollidaysburg in 1843, doubtless the same man who constructed the car on which the "Hit or Miss" was carried over the Portage.

Ultimately a number of these boats were built. They began their trip on cars in Philadelphia. Thus, passengers and goods could be shipped from one end of the state to the other, over land and water, without ever leaving the canal boat. Special boat "slips" were constructed at the points where the Columbia and Philadelphia Railroad joined the canal basin in Columbia, and at the Hollidaysburg and Johnstown canal basins, so that these portable boat sections might be made water borne by running the rail car which carried them down an incline directly into the water.

Present-day remains of the Mahantango Aqueduct on the Susquehanna Division near Selinsgrove. The canal prism is clearly visible on the far bank of the creek.

Interior of Mahantango Lock (just below the aqueduct) as photographed by Walter Leuba in 1954. Handsome stone work still in excellent condition.

Canal boat building and repair yard at Selinsgrove, 1882.

A section of the West Branch Canal near Lock Haven
as it appeared in 1954, with a local paper mill drawing
on the canal for water supply.

# OTHER DIVISIONS OF THE STATE
## CANAL SYSTEM

While the "Main Line" was the principal system developed by the State for tying Pennsylvania together, east to west, there were also other State constructed and operated divisions to supplement the Main Line, connecting with it, either directly or indirectly.

Clark's Ferry Bridge, about 1890, looking from Duncan's Island east toward Peter's Mountain. On the towpath on the down-stream side of the bridge can be seen a horse team towing a boat out of the Duncan's Island canal entrance, in the foreground. (Courtesy James A. O'Boyle)

## Susquehanna Division

The Susquehanna Division canal ran north from the outlet lock located just west of the Clark's Ferry Bridge, on Duncan's Island, along the west bank of the Susquehanna River for 39 miles to a point opposite Northumberland. Here the boats were towed to the east bank from a covered tow path bridge running into Northumberland. A slack water pool was created at this point by Shamokin Dam, which spanned the river below the junction of the north and west branches.

Canal boat in Benvenue lock at Duncan's Island, circa 1886. The lock is full and the boat is ready to proceed northward. Obviously unloaded, the boat barely clears the bridge above the lock. (Courtesy Pennsylvania Society of Professional Engineers)

The Susquehanna Division canal at Liverpool looking north. The Owens House, a familiar stopping point on the canal, can be seen at the extreme left. The old Shank Hotel, operated by the author's great grandfather, is out of the picture to the left. (Courtesy Dr. Ernest H. Coleman)

The engineers who designed and built the Susquehanna Division included: Simeon Guilford; Hother Hage, with canal office at Liverpool; Francis W. Rawle; and A. B. Waterford. Work began in 1827 and was completed in 1831. This division, with its 12 locks (90 feet x 17 feet) raising the canal boats 86 feet from the Clark's Ferry slack water pool to the Northumberland slack water pool, formed an important link with the Main Line and the canal divisions in the northern part of the state.

## North Branch Division

The North Branch of the Susquehanna Canal System commenced at the basin at Northumberland which united the Susquehanna, the North Branches and the West Branch. Including the outlet lock to the river at Northumberland, there were a total of nine locks on this section, of the standard 17 feet wide by 90 feet long type. The North Branch originally ran 55 miles to the feeder pool at Nanticoke Falls. Ground was broken at Berwick July 4, 1828 and the work on this section was completed in 1831. The important function of the North Branch was the supplying of coal to the entire Pennsylvania canal system south and west of Nanticoke, an important anthracite distribution point. Interesting features of the original North Branch Canal were: a sizeable aqueduct across Fishing Creek at Rupert, a weigh-lock at Beach Haven, and a dam across the river at Nanticoke.

An 1834 project, known as The Wyoming Extension, carried the North Branch another 17 miles northeast, past Wilkes-Barre to Pittston. A further extension of the north branch division, from Pittston along the north branch of the Susquehanna River to Athens and the New York state line, was begun in 1836, and after several long interruptions, due to financial difficulties was finally placed in operation in 1856. This section went through a rather rugged portion of the state and over the entire route (169 miles) between Northumberland and the state line 43 locks were required to overcome 334 feet of elevation. Five river dams were built to provide stretches of slack water navigation, as well as water to feed the canal sections, 29 aqueducts were constructed, and 229 bridges were built to carry local roads over the canal.

Final connection to the Erie Canal was made through an 18 mile privately-built junction canal in New York state which linked the north branch extension with Elmira. From this point the Chemung Canal ran north to Seneca Lake to make a connection with the Erie Canal.

Canal boat dry-dock at Espy (near Bloomsburg), circa 1885. The timbers at the bow and stern were steamed to provide proper curvature before application. Pennsylvania Boat Company vessels were painted white and yellow with trimmings of black and green. (Courtesy Don Shiner)

The canal boat "Towanda" was said to be the first boat to open interstate trade between Pennsylvania and New York when, in November of 1856, it took a load of anthracite coal from Pittston to Elmira. During later years of canal operation this connection permitted boats from the Pennsylvania canal system to travel as far from home as Buffalo, and Lake Champlain. After the state sold its interest in the North Branch (1858); the lower section was operated by the "Wyoming Canal Company"; the upper section by the "North Branch Canal Company."

## West Branch Division

The West Branch, also, had its southern terminus at the canal basin in Northumberland and from this point ran along the east bank of the West Branch of the Susquehanna River, north thru Muncy and west thru Williamsport, Jersey Shore and Lock Haven, to Farrandville. The West Branch Canal, started in 1828 and completed in 1835, covered a total distance of 73 miles, with 19 locks overcoming 138½ feet of vertical lockage. The primary product transported was lumber from the vast forest areas in the section of the state north and west of Williamsport.

Local residents hoped that this branch might be extended to make connection with the Allegheny River to the northwest. However, the only subsequent additions were a 4 mile state-built section known as the "Bald Eagle Cut," west of Lock Haven along Bald Eagle Creek; which was later supplemented by a 22 mile privately financed addition called the

Aqueduct on the Juniata Division at Newport. The canal furnished an avenue of transportation for all types of boats, and the towpath was an unofficial pedestrian route between towns. (Courtesy Dr. Ernest H. Coleman)

Bald Eagle and Spring Creek Navigation, making connections into Bellefonte.

A short connection known as the "Lewisburg Cut," was built in 1833 across the Susquehanna by the State to tie Lewisburg directly into the West Branch Canal System. There was also a privately-built ¾-mile connection at Muncy, known as the "Muncy Cut." After 1858, the West Branch and Susquehanna Divisions were combined and operated as the "North Branch and Susquehanna Canal Company."

The "Muncy Cut," near the Sprout-Waldron plant. Original caption to this old photo reads: "Muncy Coal Yard, Boat 502; Sis, Luce and Kate, 3 mules and 3 eyes, hard to beat!" (Courtesy Clinton H. Pressler)

Lehigh and Delaware coal boats entering the southern extremity of the Delaware Division canal at Bristol. (Courtesy Dr. Ernest H. Coleman)

## The Delaware Division

The Delaware Division of the Pennsylvania Canal was authorized by the state in 1827 and completed in 1832. It ran along the west bank of the Delaware River, from navigable water at Bristol, north to Easton, a distance of 60 miles, with 170 feet of vertical elevation being overcome by 23 lift-locks. It had no direct connection with the Main Line, serving principally as a connection between the Lehigh Canal terminus at Easton, and the Philadelphia market for the products of the Lehigh Coal and Navigation Company.

The line had nine aqueducts, 110 overhead bridges, a guard lock at Easton and a tide lock at Bristol. Water was supplied by a dam at the mouth of the Lehigh River at Easton. The sand and gravel channel of the Delaware Division leaked badly and additional water was provided to the lower section by a lifting wheel driven by a wing dam in the river at New Hope.

New York City connections with the Delaware Division were made via the Morris Canal at Phillipsburg, New Jersey, and the Delaware and Raritan Canal at Trenton, New Jersey, which reached tide water at New Brunswick.

The Delaware Division Canal is the only canal in Pennsylvania, with the possible exception of the Lehigh, which has been retained as a waterway until the present time, long after its demise as a commercial transport medium. It is today known as Roosevelt State Park. Canal buffs may ride barges out of New Hope, behind a mule team — as in the "old days."

## Beaver and Erie Division

While the Main Line Systems and the Susquehanna Divisions were being planned, the people in Erie were also clamoring for the waterway connection to which the legislature had originally committed itself, which would tie in the city of Erie with the rest of the Pennsylvania Canal System. There was great disagreement about the route to be followed. Some people in the northwestern part of the state believed the water route should proceed from a point where the Western Division aqueduct crossed the Allegheny River at Freeport, northward along the Allegheny to Franklin, then up French Creek to Meadville and from there to Erie.

The people in Pittsburgh favored a route leaving the Ohio River downstream from Pittsburgh at Beaver and running through New Castle to Conneaut Lake and Erie, by way of the Beaver and Shenango Rivers. Pittsburghers felt that if the alternate route were chosen much of the Main Line traffic at Freeport would be directed to Erie without passing through Pittsburgh.

The State act of February 25, 1826 authorized the building of the French Creek feeder connecting Conneaut Lake, Meadville and Franklin. Work on this line was started before an ultimate decision was made regarding the main north-south connection to Erie.

An Irish "digging team" with their equipment, excavating a Pennsylvania canal channel. These Irish work gangs were in constant conflict with the local authorities, as well as private citizens, along the canal route.

Pittsburgh ultimately won out, and in 1831 a program of improvement was begun along the Beaver and Shenango Rivers as far north as Pulaski. This was known as the Beaver Division (31 miles).

In February of 1836 an extension from Pulaski northward to Conneaut Lake was approved, known as the Shenango Division, bringing the system 61 miles closer to Erie. In 1838 first contracts were awarded for the Conneaut Division to make final connection between Conneaut Lake and the city of Erie, an extension of 45 miles.

The state did not complete the Erie extension. In 1843, after spending more than $4,000,000 on construction, the state turned over the whole Erie and Beaver canal project to the Erie Canal Company, headed by R. S. Reed of Erie. After investment of another half million dollars the canal was finally opened to traffic in October of 1844.

The 136 mile route of the Beaver and Erie canal required 137 locks to overcome a total rise of 977 feet. Locks were 15 x 80 feet, smaller than the Main Line standard. There were also at one time 13 dams, 9 aqueducts, 30 basins and 221 crossing road-bridges. Slackwater sections accounted for 32 miles of the route.

The Ohio River itself formed the junction between the Beaver and Erie Canal and the Main Line at Pittsburgh. Packet steamers went back and forth on the Ohio, and canal freight boats were routed from one canal to another with little inconvenience.

The Pennsylvania and Ohio Canal made connection with the Beaver and Erie Canal at New Castle, running 91 miles west to the Ohio and Erie Canal in Ohio. This Ohio connection, known as the "Cross-Cut Canal," was completed in 1840 and the primary products transported were pig iron and iron ore, as well as passengers between Pittsburgh and Cleveland.

Another short-lived connection between the Pennsylvania and Ohio canal systems was the Sandy and Beaver Canal, further south.

## The Wiconisco Canal

A small, but important canal was the Wiconisco Line, running from the east end of the Clark's Ferry Bridge northward, on the east bank of the Susquehanna to Millersburg, a distance of 12 miles. It was begun by the state in 1838 but finished, and placed in operation, by a private concern.

This line furnished an essential outlet to the coal fields of Dauphin County, via the Lykens Valley Railroad junction at Millersburg. Much traffic moved over this connection to the Main Line system.

# PRIVATELY OWNED CANALS IN PENNSYLVANIA

There were a number of sizeable privately owned canals in Pennsylvania built both before and after the decision of the Pennsylvania legislature to proceed with the "Main Line" of the Public Works of Pennsylvania. One of the oldest, the Union Canal, and its connecting Schuylkill Navigation Company, have already been described.

## Delaware and Hudson Canal

While the Delaware and Hudson Canal was a New York incorporated system, it had a considerable impact on the anthracite region of northeastern Pennsylvania, The D. & H. evolved when two Swiss brothers, William and Maurice Wurtz of Philadelphia sold a group of New York financiers on the idea of building a railroad and canal directly from the Carbondale coal region to the Hudson River near Kingston to bring anthracite coal into New York City.

The Delaware and Hudson Canal was incorporated in 1823 and completed in 1829. It connected Eddyville, just off the Hudson River near Kingston, with Honesdale in Pennsylvania, a distance of 108 miles by canal. To reach Carbondale, a 16-mile inclined-plane railroad was added. The canal was 4 feet deep, from 32 to 36 feet in width and included 107 locks, 76 feet in length by 9½ feet wide, overcoming a total change elevation of 950 feet on the uphill, downhill route. Some years after it began operation, the company replaced certain of its "at grade" river crossings with aqueducts, and hired John Roebling, the suspension-aqueduct expert, for much of the work.

John Roebling built this 600-foot long aqueduct for the D. & H. Canal crossing of the Delaware River at Lackawaxen in 1849. It was one of the first suspension structures built by Roebling (who later designed the Brooklyn Bridge) and is still in use today as a toll-bridge.

Delaware and Hudson Canal basin at Honesdale, about 1890. (Courtesy Richard Steinmetz.)

One of Roebling's most interesting projects for the D. & H. was the double-crossing over both the Lackawaxen and Delaware Rivers near their junction. Formerly a dam-created, slack-water crossing of the Delaware River only, the D. & H. had problems with the river raftsmen, who sued continually for damages incurred while crossing the D. & H. dam, and who were in constant conflict with the rope ferry crossing of D. & H. canal boats, at right angles to their line of travel.

Roebling began work on this double-aqueduct crossing, at a combined cost of $60,400. The two aqueducts were completed and opened in the Spring of 1849. The Lackawaxen aqueduct was a fairly easy two-span suspension crossing, whereas the Delaware aqueduct had four spans for a total length of 600 feet. The cable supports on the sides of the aqueduct contained 2150 wire strands each and were 8½ inches in diameter. Width of the canal channel was 19 feet.

So well was the Delaware Aqueduct constructed that after the abandonment of the D. & H. canal (in 1899) it was converted into a highway crossing and is still in use today.

Roebling was commissioned to build two more sizable aqueducts, one crossing the Neversink River, and the other at the High Falls crossing of the Rondout Creek.

There were two unique inclined-plane railroads serving the Delaware and Hudson Canal. One was the Delaware and Hudson Gravity Railroad, part of the original canal-rail system, to transport coal from the mines at

58

Carbondale to the western terminus of the canal at Honesdale; and later, a separate enterprise known as the "Pennsylvania Coal Company Gravity Railroad," connecting the Susquehanna North Branch Canal near Pittston, with the Delaware and Hudson Canal at Hawley. The former was always part of the D. & H. Company; the latter a D. & H. supplier after 1850.

The Carbondale-Honesdale Gravity Road, completed in 1829, originally consisted of five inclined planes up the steep, west side of the Moosic Mountains to Rix's Gap and three more inclined planes down the Honesdale side. Planes were numbered "One to Eight" from the west end. A change of elevation of 950 feet was overcome on the west; 970 feet on the east. The rails were wooden, with iron-strap topping, and chains were initially used to raise and lower the cars on the planes, later replaced by hemp ropes, and finally — wire cables. Since an up-bound train of cars was always balanced against a down-bound train on the planes, trackage was saved by using only one track on each plane, with a double-track "turnout" (with appropriate automatic switches) halfway up each plane for the cars to pass, in opposite directions. Power had to be applied by means of stationary steam power plants to Planes Number One to Five, as the heavy, loaded coal cars from the mines were boosted up the west side of the mountians, balanced against the "empties" coming down. However, on the east side, with the loaded cars out-weighing the "empties" it was necessary only to supply braking power to the plane mechanism.

As the coal business of the company increased in New York, the original Gravity Road became overloaded. Hence a completely separate empty-car return line was built over the Moosic 1844-56, with stationary

Canal boat crossing Roebling's two-span aqueduct across the Lackawaxen River on the Delaware and Hudson Canal. (Collection of Jim Shaughnessy)

power plants (some using water power, rather than steam) giving both loaded and empty cars a "boost" to higher elevation, and letting them coast downhill between planes. When the Gravity was finally shut down, it had a total of twenty-eight water or steam powered planes operating from Olyphant (to which it had been extended) to Carbondale, to Honesdale.

In 1847, the Delaware and Hudson Canal Company, contracted with the Wyoming Coal Association to form a separate company, which became known as the Pennsylvania Coal Company. The prime objective of the new firm was to transport coal from the Nanticoke area of the Susquehanna North Branch, and coal fields between, overland to Hawley on the D. & H. Canal. Here the coal was to be sold to the D.& H. Canal Company, and it was part of the original agreement that the new Pennsylvania Coal Company was also to be charged a special toll rate for use of the canal into New York. It was on the latter point that legal difficulties developed, and resulting strained relationship between the two companies led to early termination of the entire operation.

However, the Pennsylvania Coal Company did build a Gravity Railroad approximately forty miles long connecting Port Griffith on the Susquehanna, through Dunmore, to Hawley on the Lackawaxen River. It was quite similar in operation to the D. & H. (improved) Gravity Railroad, with a total of twenty-two inclined planes, most of them operated by steam, but four using water wheels as a power source.

The D. & H. Canal reached the peak of its operation, in terms of tons of coal shipped, about 1883. From this time on its business declined until it was finally phased out of existence, at the turn of the century.


## The Lehigh Canal

One of the earliest, and without doubt one of the most successful financial enterprises in Pennsylvania was the Lehigh Canal, running 72 miles from White Haven in the upper Lehigh River Valley to Easton, where the Lehigh River joins the Delaware.

The success of this canal, which was chartered in 1818 and which continued full operation for the next 113 years, was due solely to the dogged determination and inventive genius of a Quaker from Philadelphia named Josiah White.

As a young man of 29, Josiah had in 1810 acquired ownership of the Schuylkill Falls at Philadelphia and had developed a dam and double-lock combination there for navigation purposes. Also, in partnership with one Erskine Hazard, he had harnessed the water power from the dam to operate two manufacturing plants—one for wrought iron nails, and the other for wire.

An old print showing canal boats and freight cars being loaded with coal at Mauch Chunk (now Jim Thorpe) on the Lehigh Canal.

In his manufacturing of nails and wire, White used a soft, sulphur coal from Virginia for smelting. When the War of 1812 broke out, both White's plants began operating at top speed. The British naval blockade of Philadelphia, however, soon cut off the Virginia coal source and the two plants were forced to shut down. White and his partner turned to "black rock" from the Lehighton area of eastern Pennsylvania as a fuel source. Because of the great difficulty in igniting and maintaining a fire with this black rock, in the furnaces designed for soft coal, no one took the fuel seriously, until Josiah White, quite by accident, discovered that forced draft solved the problem and produced furnace temperatures never dreamed possible with soft coal. He bought every boat load of "black rock" which found its tortuous and uncertain way into Philadelphia via the Lehigh and Delaware Rivers.

With the end of the war, interest in "hard coal" subsided in favor of Virginia soft coal once again, leaving Josiah White as the sole champion of anthracite in the Philadelphia area. Looking for a means of transporting this new fuel into Philadelphia from the upper Lehigh region,

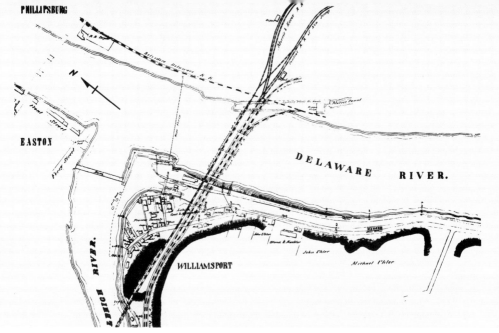

Junction of Lehigh Canal, Morris Canal and Delaware Division at Easton.
(Courtesy Pennsylvania Canal Society.)

Josiah approached the owners of the Schuylkill Navigation, then under construction. Their proposed transportation charges were so high that Josiah decided to establish a competitive system along the Lehigh River.

With the encouragement of Colonel Weiss of Lehighton, White and his partner, Erskine Hazard, petitioned the state for permission to make the Lehigh River navigable. A bill was passed by the State Legislature, March 20, 1818 granting them "permisison to build a slack water navigation by locks, dams or any devices" which they chose and when the downstream passage was complete they were to be permitted to charge toll. It was agreed that this was to be a one-way, or "descending," navigation, to be completed by 1824. It was stipulated also that a return passage, i.e., "ascending" navigation, was to be completed by 1838.

At the age of 36, with virtually no spare capital in hand other than the somewhat questionable assets of the "Schuylkill Falls" enterprises at Philadelphia, Josiah and his partner were nevertheless able to persuade various financiers in Philadelphia to invest in two companies, one known as the "Lehigh Coal Company" and the other as the "Lehigh Navigation Company." The first company was to mine the coal and the other to transport it to Philadelphia by water. The two companies combined, February 22, 1822, into the "Lehigh Coal and Navigation Company."

This company is today still operating from headquarters in Bethlehem, Pa., under the name "Lehigh Navigation—Dodson Company."

Josiah White was a natural born inventor. Many of the appliances and devices which he developed and built for mining, loading and transporting coal from the top of Summit Hill, first to his operating base, Mauch Chunk, and then to Philadelphia, have yet to be duplicated anywhere else in the world. One of his first major inventions, in connection with his navigation system, was the "Bear Trap Lock" for which he took out patent papers in 1819. This was a one-way lock, operated by an ingenious water-valving arrangement and hydrostatic pressure which allowed a surge of water to carry the boat in the lock down a flume to the next lower slack water pool.

This lock was different from anything else either in Europe or America and worked with highly satisfactory results. The invention was hailed as a revolutionary contribution to navigation. In June of 1820 Josiah floated his first fleet of coal boats from Mauch Chunk (a modification of the Indian name for "Bear Mountain") to Philadelphia. The boats were dis-assembled in Philadelphia and sold for lumber. The Lehigh Navigation was officially open for regular business in 1823, a full year ahead of the required deadline.

Josiah next turned his attention to the problem of more rapid transportation across the nine-mile stretch from the coal mine on Summit Hill to the Lehigh River at Mauch Chunk. With true pioneer spirit Josiah White decided to build a railroad, *the first coal railroad in the U.S.A.*, from Summit Hill to Mauch Chunk. Ground was broken for the line January 1, 1827 and it was completed in April of the same year. The downhill trip with loaded coal cars, or "wagons," was made entirely by gravity. Each wagon carried a ton and a half of coal. A brake, attached to a cable, was the only control provided. One driver could manage a complete gang of wagons hitched together. The system worked beautifully and was soon dubbed the "Gravity Road." Mules were used to tow the empty cars up to the mine after each down-hill trip. Special "mule cars" were included on the down-hill run to bring the animals back to Mauch Chunk. To save time, the mules were also fed during the ride down. The descending cars made the nine mile journey in 20 minutes, an unbelievable speed for the times!

In June of 1829 the two-way section of the regular "Lehigh Canal" was completed. No longer was it necesary for arks or boats going down the bear trap lock system to be dismantled and sold in Philadelphia. Now the boats could be returned upstream via the canal. The entire project had taken only two years to complete, from Mauch Chunk to Easton. The Delaware Division of the Pennsylvania Canal System, authorized in 1827 for completion in 1829, was not opened for its entire length until 1832, much to the annoyance of the impatient manager of the Lehigh Canal System.

Josiah White turned his attention in the meantime to a possible market for coal in New York via the Morris Canal, which was then being constructed to join the Lehigh Canal at Easton. With admirable fore-sight Josiah White had made the locks on his Lehigh Canal large enough to handle boats of 150 ton capacity and he urged the Morris Canal builders to do likewise. However, despite all his pleas, the Morris Canal was built with locks comparable to those of the Union Canal and hence was handicapped from the very outset.

With water routes finally completed to both New York and Phila-delphia, Josiah White now turned his attention westward, envisioning a combination canal and rail route to make connections with the Sus-quehanna North Branch Canal. His first move in this direction was to provide a canal from Mauch Chunk north to the town of White Haven (named in his honor) along a particularly rugged stretch of the Lehigh. All the experts said this would require locks of such tremendous lift that the project was out of the question. Nevertheless Josiah tackled the job, building a series of locks larger than any yet in existence in this country. They were 20 feet in width, 100 feet in length with a maximum lift of a full thirty feet. The Canal Commissioners, who inspected the works in 1838, glowed in their praise: "We passed through a succession of the largest, best-constructed and most easily managed locks within our knowledge and of such magnitude as greatly to exceed any public works in the whole United States. We were filled with admiration and delight when we examined these stupendous works, which have made the Lehigh from a shallow, wild, useless stream into a calm and beautiful river, suited for all purposes of navigation, either for trade or pleasure."

Josiah White's final achievement, to tie his entire navigation and transportation system together from east to west, was the "Lehigh and Susquehanna Railroad" completed in 1841, which carried freight over the mountains 25 miles from White Haven on the Lehigh to Wilkes-Barre on the Susquehanna. To lift the loaded cars out of Wyoming Valley on the north end of the route he used a series of three inclined planes, known as the "Ashley planes," run by powerful stationary engines similar in design to those on the Allegheny Portage Railroad. These planes were said to have the highest lift of any in the world. The rail line also included an 1800-foot tunnel north of White Haven.

Passenger car ascending Mount Jefferson on the Switchback Railroad near Mauch Chunk. Note the "booster," or safety car, at the rear. The descending track is shown beneath the car.

Inclined plane on the Switchback Railroad at Mount Pisgah. The entire double track mechanism was operated from a stationary power plant at the top of the mountain.

Present day appearance of a lock on the Delaware Division canal near New Hope. This canal is currently being maintained as a public park by the Pennsylvania Department of Environmental Resources.

Disaster struck Josiah White's enterprises in 1841 when a tremendous flood rolled down the Lehigh Valley, with great loss of life, destroying most of the Lehigh Navigation System, portions of his coal and iron works and virtually all of the beautifully constructed locks of the Lehigh Valley Canal. Such a catastrophe would have ruined a lesser man, but Josiah White, with fierce determination, within four months rebuilt enough of his navigation system to get back into operation, at least to Philadelphia, and shortly thereafter restored most of his canal system to its original condition. The White Haven section was ultimately abandoned.

But the transportation medium for which White became most famous was the so-called "Switch Back Railroad." This amazing system replaced the "Gravity Road" between Summit Hill and Mauch Chunk in 1846 and operated solely by gravity over 17 of its 18 miles of track. Like a "roller-coaster," the cars were given a boost in elevation at two points on the up-grade by means of a 2322 foot long by 664 foot high inclined plane up Mt. Pisgah, and a 2070 foot long by 462 foot high plane at Mt. Jefferson. At the foot of each of these planes, a "booster car," which Josiah White named his Safety Car, came out of a pit beneath the track and pushed the passenger or coal cars up the incline. The motive power for the booster was a stationary steam engine at the head of each plane driving a 28 foot diameter drum which reeled in two Swedish iron bands, each 7½ inches wide, to which the boosters were attached. At the head of each plane the cars were free to coast, with no control other than a brake on the wheels. By this means the cars attained an elevation of 1500 feet above sea level on top of Mt. Pisgah and 1660 feet at Mt. Jefferson. The down-hill ride between planes, and particularly on the

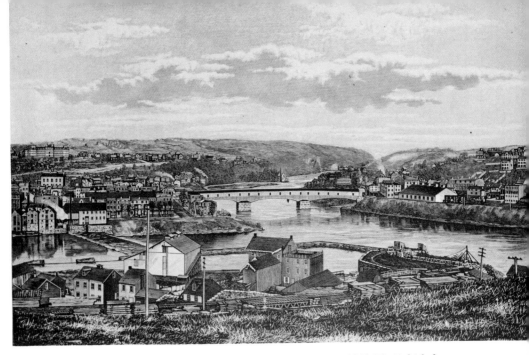

Junction of the Lehigh and Delaware Canals at Easton, circa. 1845. The Lehigh dam is at the left, feeder basin for the Delaware Canal at the center, outlet lock to the Morris Canal at the right. In the background is Timothy Palmer's covered bridge connecting Easton and Phillipsburg. (Courtesy Hugh Moore, Jr.)

A "Winding Bridge" to switch the towpath from one side of the canal to the other, without unhitching the horses.

Present- day appearance of Lock Twelve on the Susquehanna and Tidewater Canal along the lower Susquehanna. Masonry still in excellent condition.

A freight boat entering a Weight Lock to check its pay-load, for toll charge.

9-mile return descent from Summit Hill to Mauch Chunk, was quiet, as fast as the brakeman deemed safe, and altogether awe-inspiring and thrilling to the thousands of tourists who flocked to the Lehigh Valley each summer to ride the famous "Switch-Back," between loads of coal. This novel system continued operations until 1932.

Josiah White died November 15, 1850, but the works of his hands lived on for many years.

The Delaware Division of the Pennsylvania Canal System was sold by the State to the Erie and Sunbury Railroad in 1858. The Lehigh Coal and Navigation Company acquired control of this canal line on a 99 year lease basis, several years later. The old Delaware Division then continued to operate as part of the Lehigh Coal and Navigation Company system until 1931, when it was reacquired in part by the State of Pennsylvania. In 1940 the balance of the Delaware Division was conveyed to the State and is called "Roosevelt State Park."

Today, also, a three-mile section of the Lehigh Canal above Easton has been fully restored and is known as the "Hugh Moore Park." A mule-drawn canal boat is available in summer, traveling between several of the restored locks.

## The Susquehanna and Tidewater Canal

No account of the Pennsylvania canals would be complete without a reference to the Susquehanna and Tidewater Canal. For years before the canal-building era, the Susquehanna River had been an avenue for trade between the southern counties of Pennsylvania and Baltimore. Because of difficult navigation, most river shipping had been downstream on arks or flatboats, which were dismantled at their destination. Lower Susquehanna navigation was improved somewhat when the one-mile Conewago Canal was opened in 1797 around Conewago Falls, near York Haven, but the going was still rough.

Baltimore needed the raw materials which Pennsylvania could provide, and after the anthracite coal regions were developed the city was particuarly anxious for a shorter route to the eastern Pennsylvania coal

Ruins of one of the Susquehanna and Tidewater locks about 1/5 mile north of Shenk's Ferry. (Courtesy G. Ross Bond)

69

Appearance of the entrance to the Susquehanna and Tidewater canal at Wrightsville, looking south, about 1885. When the Columbia-Wrightsville bridge was burned during the Civil War a "side-wheeler" steam tug called "The Columbia" was substituted for mule power to pull the boats across the river. This tug is shown to the left of the photograph. Note the arched bridge in the background to allow the mules to cross from the mainland to the tow-path. (Courtesy John G. Redmond)

mines. For about ten years, during the canal boom of the 1820's, Maryland carried on negotiations with the State of Pennsylvania for a joint canal to open up the lower Susquehanna. Philadelphians objected, feeling that it would divert much of their own western trade to Baltimore. However, when the Chesapeake and Delaware canal was completed in 1829, Philadelphians perceived that the proposed canal could be part of an all-water route from Philadelphia to Columbia at less expense than the overland Philadelphia-Columbia railway, and so acquiesced.

In 1835 Pennsylvania granted a charter to the Susquehanna Canal Company, to build a canal from Columbia to the State line. Maryland had already chartered the Tidewater Canal Company to build her part of the canal from Havre de Grace, north. The two companies were later united under the name "Susquehanna and Tidewater Canal Company."

Excavation began in 1836. It was decided that the west bank of the Susquehanna was a more feasible route for the canal. Hence, the river was dammed below Columbia and Wrightsville to form a pool for the canal boats to cross from the Main Line basin at Columbia and also to feed water into the new canal. The Susquehanna and Tidewater entrance basin was located at Wrightsville and the canal was constructed 43 miles south to Havre de Grace, Maryland with approximately two-thirds of the route in Pennsylvania and the remaining one-third in Maryland. The canal was put into operation in 1840.

A most interesting wooden covered bridge with a double-deck tow path along the downstream side was constructed between Wrightsville and Columbia, permitting mule teams to proceed both east and west on the bridge without interfering with each other. This bridge, incidentally, was burned during the Civil War by retreating Union forces when the Confederates threatened Philadelphia prior to the battle at Gettysburg. Subsequently steam tugs were substituted to tow the boats back and forth between the two canal systems.

Twenty-nine locks were built to overcome an elevation of 231 feet between Havre de Grace and Wrightsville. Avoiding the now obvious error of some of the earlier canals, such as the Union, in building their locks too narrow and too small, locks on the S. & T. were built 17 feet in width and 170 feet in length, thus permitting single boats of 150 tons capacity or tandem boats up to 300 tons capacity per pair to pass the locks easily. The canal channel was designed 50 feet wide at water level by 5½ to 6 feet deep. There was a weigh lock located at York Furnace where tolls were charged. Average dimensions of the double (or tandem) boats using the canal system were 65 feet in length, 16 feet in width and 8 feet in depth, drawing approximately 5 feet of water fully loaded.

Original highway and tow-path bridge between Columbia and Wrightsville, from the Wrightsville end. Note the double deck, canopy covered tow-path arrangement. This bridge was burned in 1863 to prevent a Confederate invasion of Lancaster. (Courtesy Gerald P. Smeltzer)

Materials shipped on this canal were coal, lumber, grain and iron, much of it south-bound to Baltimore, and also to Philadelphia, by way of the Chesapeake and Delaware Canal.

Tugs were used to tow the boats from the outlet lock at Havre de Grace to the port of Baltimore. Mule teams for the Baltimore bound boats generally waited at Havre de Grace for the boats to make the return trip north. However, if the boats were bound for Philadelphia by way of the Chesapeake and Delaware canal the mule teams were stowed on board and put back on the tow paths as necessary. In some cases the teams drew their boats all the way to the port of New York, via the New Jersey canal connections previously mentioned.

On the Susquehanna and Tidewater there were a total of four dams feeding the canal, five culverts, 18 overhead bridges, 33 waste-weirs and 6 aqueducts. A long reach of canal, unbroken by locks for five miles below Wrightsville became known as the "Five-Mile-Long Level" and to this day the area retains the name "Long Level' although the origin of the name has long since been forgotten.

Assets of the original Susquehanna and Tidewater Canal Company were sold to the Reading Railroad in 1872. The Reading continued to operate the canal until May of 1894 to make connections with its railroad lines running into Columbia. Prime commodity was coal, bound for the port of Baltimore.

## The Conestoga Navigation Company

Various individuals had attempted to make the Conestoga Creek navigable between Lancaster and the Susquehanna River. Several companies had been chartered for this purpose, the first in 1806 and the second in 1820, but nothing was done and the charters became inactive. May 15th, 1824, however, there was a mass meeting at the Lancaster Court House and a petition sent to the State for permission to take definite action on improvements to the Conestoga.

On March 3, 1825 an act "authorizing the governor to incorporate the Conestoga Navigation Company" was approved by the State legislature. Local commissioners were appointed and authorized to sell stock.

The section considered for navigation ran from Reigart's Landing in southeast Lancaster to Safe Harbor, on the Susquehanna. Simeon Guil-

Typical lock and dam combination on the Conestoga Navigation system. Note that the lock is lined with wood planking.

ford, who had prior experience on various canal projects, was engaged as the engineer.

The meandering Conestoga Creek ran 18 miles between the extremities of the proposed improvements. It was decided to make the entire route slack-water navigation, with nine dam-lock combinations.

The locks were designed 22 feet wide by 100 feet long. Ponds between dams were planned with a minimum depth of 4 feet and an average width of 200 feet. Construction of the whole project was awarded to Caleb Hammill, a New York state contractor, at a bid price of $53,240.

The company was beset with financial difficulties from the outset. A severe freshet on the Conestoga in 1827 destroyed several of the completed dams and damaged others. The job was finally completed, in early 1828, and navigation began. The opening of the Susquehanna and Tidewater Canal in 1840 gave the Conestoga Navigation the opportunity of making direct connections with Baltimore and the Main Line canal system. A dam was constructed across the river below Safe Harbor and boats from the Conestoga could then be towed across the Susquehanna to an outlet lock on the S. & T. at Lockport.

In spite of this, the history of the Conestoga Navigation Company is one of financial difficulties, sheriff's sales and "washouts." The dams were of some value as a power source for various mills along the stream, but operation of the navigation phase of the system was never profitable and the company went through several changes of ownership before the works were abandoned for navigation, in 1865.

# The Leiper Canal

From about 1829 to 1852 a several-mile section of Crum Creek, near Chester, Pa., was canalized by George C. Leiper, who used this means of transporting stone from his quarry at Springfield to tidewater on the Delaware River at Eddystone. The system included three locks, through which ran flat-bottom boats of eight tons capacity. The canal replaced an earlier tramway (or railroad) built in 1808, using wooden cars with flanged iron wheels, powered by oxen.

## The Codorus Navigation Company

The Codorus Navigation Company, with headquarters at York, Pa., was formed May 5, 1829, with stock offered for public subscription. C. A. Barnitz was president of the company and a vigorous promoter. So great was the local interest in the project that much of the estimated $84,850 construction cost was subscribed in the first few months— $10,500 worth of stock being purchased in a single day. The original plans called for eight miles of slack-water pools and three miles of canals to make the Codorus Creek navigable from York to the Susquehanna River above Chestnut Ripples. Simeon Guilford, a canal engineer already involved in design of the Conestoga Navigation and other canals, was retained as the company engineer. Ten dams and thirteen locks, including 2 guard locks, were planned. The locks were constructed 95 feet in length by 18 feet wide, with an average lift of about 7 feet. Presumably connection was to be made by means of the river, with the Main Line Canal basin via the outlet lock at Columbia.

A newspaper item dated March 27, 1832 reads: "The Codorus Navigation will be finished in the course of a few months. The tow path is already made to the head of the Codorus Forge Dam, within a mile and a half of the River and the whole work is progressing rapidly and surely." On July 4, 1832, "The Farmer" of York carried this item: "The managers of the Codorus Navigation Company announce to the stockholders and the public generally, the completion of the first section of the works (a distance of about three miles) and will open it this morning. The new passenger boat 'Codorus' (70 feet in length and carrying 150 passengers) will start from Maine Street Bridge at 9:30 AM, 12 (noon) and 2 and 4 PM. Fare going and returning, 25 cents. The boat during this day will be under the direction of Captain Jacob Barnitz." Another vessel specifically built for this canal at the same time was the "Pioneer," operated by Gottlieb Zeigle, James Schall and Daniel Ford. These two

Artist's drawing of York, circa 1840, looking south from the Harrisburg road (now North George Street). The Codorus Navigation channel can be seen in the foreground.

boats originally ran excursions between York and Barnitz's Springs. The Pioneer offered special cruises in addition to the regular run at 5 PM Tuesday, Thursday and Saturday: "On all other days of the week the Pioneer may be chartered, and the individual or company chartering the boat will have the privilege of appointing the hour of departure and return."

Full operation on the Codorus Navigation system did not commence until 1833 and included arks and rafts which still found their way down the Susquehanna River from the north. The first ark arrived in York in 1833 with 40,000 feet of lumber and 100 passengers aboard. The York papers of that year listed a few boats or arks arriving with logs, shingles, stone, coal, staves, boards, etc. Subsequently little mention is made in the local press of the activities of this short-lived canal.

The original plans stated: "At the outlet (on the Susquehanna River) a canal will be required along the shore of the Susquehanna to the still water above Chestnut Ripples." This connection was apparently planned to make easy access for the down-river rafts and arks, into the Codorus Navigation system, and York. Today there is still visual evidence that this extension, north of the point where the Codorus joins the Susquehanna, was partly constructed and then abandoned.

The York and Maryland Railroad was completed from York to Baltimore in 1838 and in 1840 the Wrightsville, York and Gettysburg Railroad started operations. It appears obvious that the Codorus Navigation Company died quietly, as a direct result of too much train smoke, about 1850, or shortly thereafter.

# The Monongahela Navigation Company

The only section of Pennsylvania's slack water and canal navigation of the 1800's still in full operation today is the Monongahela Navigation between Pittsburgh and Fairmont, West Virginia.

Originally a private venture, the Monongahela Navigation Company was formed March 24, 1817 by act of the state legislature authorizing George Sutton, Anthony Beelan, Thomas Baird and Associates, of Pittsburgh, to issue 1600 shares of stock for construction of 16 dams with by-pass locks along the Monongahela to form a slack water navigation.

The company was given 25 years to complete the work to the point where the Cheat River joined the Monongahela, close to the Pennsylvania-West Virginia line. A highly successful financial operation, the Monongahela Navigation easily met the State deadline and extended its operations as far south as Fairmont, W. Va. The principal product transported downstream to Pittsburgh was bituminous coal from the West Virginia coal mines.

In 1880, the company was paying 12% dividends on a capital investment of $1,115,000 and 3,193,000 tons of coal were transported that year.

In 1897 the Federal Government assumed possession of the works, by condemnation proceedings, and the U. S. Corps of Engineers is today operating the system, toll-free, to carriers of products of the Monongahela Valley. The various dams and locks in the system have been increased in size, and decreased in number. In 1965 there were only 12 dam-lock combinations between Fairmont and Pittsburgh, with an average lift of 12.2 feet. The highest is the Hildebrand Dam-Lock, south of Morgantown, W. Va., with a lift of 21 feet. Eight of the locks are in Pennsylvania and four in West Virginia. The five downstream locks are double, two locks side by side, and the balance are single. The complete length of the navigation from the Golden Triangle to Kingmont, W. Va., just south of Fairmont, is 130.7 miles, with a total change in elevation of 146.8 feet being overcome by the locks.

Principal traffic over the Monongahela Navigation System today consists of barges motivated by tugs, still carrying soft coal from the West Virginia mines to the steel mills and other industries of the Pittsburgh area.

A short-lived connection to the Monongahela Navigation was the Youghiogheny Navigation Company, an 18.5-mile slack-water operation between McKeesport and West Newton. It had two dam-locks overcoming a river fall of 26.67 feet. It began operations in 1850 but was destroyed by a flood in January of 1865.

Typical single lock on the Monongahela Navigation system. The gates are power driven. The system is currently operated by the U. S. Corps of Engineers.

## LIFE ON THE CANALS

There will never again be a period in the travel history of this country quite as colorful or as unique as the canal-boat era, which reached its peak in the 1850's and continued on a gradually diminishing scale until about 1900. The canal boat traveler found himself, particularly at night or on rainy days, thrown into extremely intimate contact with his fellow travelers in the crowded cabin. All boats were animal-drawn. Mules were found most suitable for the heavy freight boats although oxen were in use in some areas. The "Packets," or passenger-carrying boats, which generally moved at the maximum speed permissible on the canals, found horses speedier towing animals. The State set a speed limit of four miles per hour, as higher speeds created a backwash which undercut the earthen canal banks. Some boats carried their own spare teams on board, generally forward, which added somewhat to the variety of odors on the boat. Two to three animals were used as a towing team, depending upon the boat size, with a "driver" on shore with the team and a "steersman" at the tiller to guide the boat. The more prosperous packets sported a crew of five or six with a captain, but on some of the freighters the "crew" consisted of a steersman (who was also captain) and a mule driver.

The "canalers" were a hardy lot, and although certain rules and regulations existed about right of way on the canals, it was usually the canal boats with the toughest crews that cleared the locks first. (It was at the locks that the most frequent bottlenecks occurred.) Some of the competing packet boats literally raced each other from one to the next. The lock tender was supposed to decide, in the event two boats arrived at the same time, which was to be given preference, but usually the boat whose crew could lick the other (and often did) was on its way while the other waited.

Lock gates were generally V-shaped, one pair at each end of the lock, with the point of the V upstream. These gates were manually opened and closed by means of "balance beams" or long arms on each gate, operated from the banks by the lock tender, often with assistance from the boat crew. The lock gates could not be opened except when the pressure of the water was equalized on both sides. This equalization was accomplished by means of small sluice gates in the lock gates themselves which could be slid up or turned by means of rods that projected above the balance beams. Later, drop-type lock gates were substituted at the upper ends of some locks, which permitted more rapid passage of the boats. These gates were hinged at the bottom of the lock and folded down into the lock bed, on the upstream side, permitting the boats to pass over them.

Operation of the locks early developed into an art, and several English authors noted with surprise the speed with which boats were passed through. Captain Marryat in a Diary in America (London, 1839) wrote: "When the boat had entered the lock, and the gate was closed upon her, the water was let off with a rapidity which considerably affected her level, and her bows pointed downwards. I timed one lock with a fall of fifteen feet. From the time the gate was closed behind us until the lower one was opened for our egress, was exactly one minute and a quarter; and the boat sank down so rapidly as to give you the idea that she was scuttled and sinking." It took a boat going downstream about five minutes to get through a lock; upstream it took longer. Normally boats could be passed through the locks at eight-minute intervals.

The driver on shore was the "forager" for the crew. If a fat hen from some farmer's hen house wandered too close to the tow path it was only natural that it should wind up in the dinner pot on board. Ripe fruit near the tow path seldom was harvested by the owner. The top rails on fences adjoining the tow path also had a mysterious way of disappearing on cold nights, when the canal boat stove was low in fuel.

Preparing the local populace for the opening of the Eastern Division the following year, a reporter for the "Harrisburg Reporter" on June 2, 1832 described the boats of David Leech of Armstrong County, on which he had traveled on the Western Division: "These boats are constructed

"Canalers" replenishing their galley supplies from a convenient farm yard.

according to the most approved plan of those used on the New York and Erie Canal. The largest are 79 feet long, and will carry 25 passengers and 30 tons of freight, drawn by two horses. The apartments are these: A ladies' cabin in the bow of the boat, calculated for eight persons. This cabin is handsomely decorated, and has tables, chairs and beds for that number of persons, and is as neat and comfortable as such rooms usually are in steam boats. The next room is what is called the 'midships,' containing the freight. Next is the gentlemen's room, large enough for all passengers; this room besides a bar with the choicest liquors, is calculated for a table, at which all the passengers breakfast, dine and sup, and contains beds and bunks for all the male passengers. The last room is the kitchen, at the steerage, where cooking is done in superior style."

Women canal travelers were somewhat critical of the "neat and comfortable" conditions described above, if we are to judge from the writings of Harriet Beecher Stowe, famous American authoress of "Uncle Tom's Cabin,' who traveled the Main Line in 1841: " 'There's the boat!' exclaims a passenger in the omnibus as we are rolling down from the Pittsburgh Mansion House to the canal—'Where?' exclaim a dozen of voices, and forthwith a dozen heads go out of the window. 'Why, down there under that bridge, don't you see those lights!' 'What, that little thing?' exclaims an inexperienced traveller, 'Dear me! we can't half of us get into it!' 'Indeed,' says an old hand in the business—'I think you'll find it will hold us and a dozen more loads like us.' 'Impossible!' say some. 'You'll see,' say the initiated; and as soon as you get out you do see, and hear

Canal trade boats were popular with the housewives but not with the local merchants. They usually sent a rider ahead to prepare the townspeople for their arrival.

too, what seems like a general breaking loose from the Tower of Babel, amid a perfect hail storm of trunks, boxes, valises, carpet bags.

"Amusing is the look of dismay which each newcomer gives to the confined quarters that present themselves. Those who were so ignorant of the power of compression as to suppose the boat scarce large enough to contain them and theirs, find, with dismay, a respectable colony of old ladies, babies, mothers, big baskets, and carpet bags already established. 'Mercy on us!' says one, after surveying the little room, about ten feet long and six high, 'Where are we all to sleep to-night?'

"Then there is the 'turning out scene,' when the whole caravan's ejected into the gentlemen's cabin, that the beds may be made. The red curtains are put down, and in solemn silence all, the last mysterious preparations begin. At length, it is announced that all is ready. Forthwith the whole company rush back, and find the walls embellished by a series of little shelves, about a foot wide, each furnished with a mattress and bedding, and hooked to the ceiling by a very suspiciously slender cord—Direful are the ruminations and exclamations of inexperienced travellers . . as they eye these very equivocal accommodations. 'What, sleep up there!—I won't sleep on one of those top shelves I know. The cords will certainly break.' The chambermaid here takes up the conversation and solemnly assures them that such an accident is not to be thought of at all, that it is a natural impossibility . . Points of location being after a while adjusted, comes the last struggle. Everybody wants to take off their bonnet, to look for their shawl, to find their cloak, to get their carpet-bag, and all set about it with such zeal that nothing can

Confusion in the ladies compartment, as described by Harriet Beecher
Stowe.

Male passengers drew lots for bunks on the packet boats at night,
"three high".

Meals on board the Packet Boats, according to Charles Dickens, were pretty much the same fare — morning, noon and night.

"Low bridge! Everybody down!"

be done. 'Ma'am, you're on my foot,' says one. 'Will you please to move, ma'am,' says somebody who is gasping and struggling behind you. 'Move!' you echo. 'Indeed, I should be very glad to, but I don't see much prospect of it.' 'Chambermaid!' calls a lady who is struggling among a heap of carpet bags and children at one end of the cabin. 'Ma'am!' echoes the poor chambermaid, who is wedged fast in a similar position at the other. 'Where's my cloak, chambermaid?' 'I'd find it, ma'am, if I could move.' 'Chambermaid, my basket!' 'Chambermaid, my parasol!' 'Chambermaid, a glass of water!' 'Mamma, they push me so!' 'Hush, child, crawl under there and lie still till I can undress you.'

"At last, however, the various distresses are over, the babies sunk to sleep, and even that much-enduring being, the chambermaid, seeks out some corner for repose. Tired and drowsy, you are just sinking into a dose, when bang! goes the boat against the sides of a lock, ropes scrape, men run and shout, and up fly the heads of all the top-shelfites, who are generally the more juvenile and airy part of the company.

" 'What's that? What's that?' flies from mouth to mouth, and forthwith they proceed to awaken their respective relations. 'Mother—Aunt Hannah!—do wake up—What is this awful noise?' 'Oh, only a lock!' 'Pray, be still!' groan out the sleepy members from below.

"Again all is still—you hear only the trampling of the horses, the rippling of the rope in the water, and sleep again is stealing over you. You dose, you dream, and all of a sudden you are startled by a cry 'Chambermaid! Wake up the lady that wants to be set ashore!'

"Up jumps chambermaid and up jumps the lady and two children, and forthwith form a committee of inquiry as to ways and means. 'Where's my bonnet?' says the lady, half awake and fumbling among the various articles of the name. 'I thought I hung it up behind the door.' 'Can't you find it?' says poor chambermaid, yawning and rubbing her eyes. 'Oh, yes, here it is,' says the lady, and then her cloak, the shawl, the gloves, the shoes, receive each a separate discussion. At last all seems ready and they begin to move off, when lo! Peter's cap is missing. The chambermaid then proceeds to turn over all the children on the floor to see if it isn't under them, in the course of which they are all most agreeably waked up and enlivened; and when everybody is broad awake and uncharitably wishing the cap and Peter, too, at the bottom of the canal, the good lady exclaims, 'Well, if this isn't lucky!—here I had it safe in my basket all the time.'—and she departs amid the—what shall I say?—execrations?—of the whole company, ladies though they be.

"Well, after this follows a hushing up and wiping up among the juvenile population, and a conversation commences from the various shelves, of a very edifying and instructive tendency—At last, however, voice after voice drops off—you fall into a most refreshing slumber—it seems that you sleep about a quarter of an hour, when the chambermaid pulls you by the sleeve. 'Will you please to get up, ma'am; we want to make the beds.' You start and stare—sure enough, the night is done! So much for sleeping on a canal boat."

Not all who kept an account of their travels on the Pennsylvania canals were professional writers. John Hamilton, a citizen of Lock Haven, Pa., kept a daily log of his voyage on a Union Canal freight boat from Pine Creek in Clinton County to Philadelphia. The trip was made in the fall of 1839, by way of the West Branch Canal, the Susquehanna Division and the Union Canal. Hamilton served as "bowsman' and the boat was captained by a John Rose. Samuel M. Simmons was in charge of supercargo, and Isaac Smith Simmons was driver. The trip took ten days going and twelve days returning. Following are excerpts from Hamilton's daily journal:

"Monday, Nov. 11, 1839.—Left Northumberland at daylight; traveled nearly a South course through the counties of Union, Perry and Juniata. Passed the towns of Sunbury, Selinsgrove and Liverpool. The canal keeps the West side of the Susquehanna River, which breaks through the range of mountains transversely. Three miles below Liverpool we passed a railroad, which runs nine miles up through Lykens Valley on the opposite side of the river. Met a packet in the morning; passed one in the evening. A little before sundown came in sight of Liverpool, a small town. A thick smoke came from all the chimneys as if all were kindling their fires at one time, perhaps for supper.

"Tuesday, Nov. 12.—Left New Buffalo, or Bachman's. Frosty morning. Course in the morning South; then Southeast. Passed out of Perry into Dauphin. Passed the Juniata Division. There was a very beautiful residence on the point of a large island* above the mouth of the Juniata. Crossed to the East side of the river. Passed the old Dauphin tannery. Took three ladies on board to go as far as Harrisburg, which point we reached at 2 o'clock. An appearance of much business going on here. Well supplied. Canal, railroad and turnpike. Four miles below Harrisburg met a locomotive, which frightened our horses into the canal and through it, breaking the towing line. The horses were stopped at a farmer's barn. Gathered up and started again, stopping for the night at Middletown. The country passed through seems fruitful and cultivated.

* Duncan's Island.

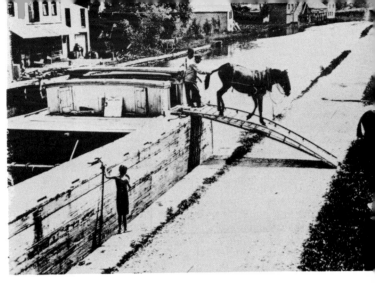

The animal stables were generally forward on the canal boats. Here a new team is being run out on the tow path. (Courtesy Canal Society of New York State)

"Wednesday, Nov. 13.—Left Middletown before day; took the Union Canal, which winds along the Swatara, the division between Dauphin and Lancaster Counties. A limestone country, hilly, but the hills low and tillable. Horses broke and ran off about one and a half miles; stopped by a boat driver; little damage done. Passed out of the limestone region into the slate; oak timber; neither hilly nor level. Plain, old-fashioned settlements. Many of the buildings log; barns thatched with straw; clay ovens; women scutching flax. Two or three o'clock we passed from Dauphin into Lebanon County. Same appearance of country. It looks like a settlement of good, old residenters, ignorant of pride. Log houses with whitewashed cracks, thatched barns; women at work out doors. Crossed the Swatara in the evening. Passed the water works and the Pine Grove feeder, which is navigable 18 or 20 miles. The water works are for throwing water into the Summit level. Went through 9 or 10 of the locks after dark. These 19 locks are all close together at the West end of the Summit level. Stopped for the night at 10 o'clock. The day has been pleasant. Traveled 34 miles.

"Thursday, Nov. 14.—Started about daylight. Passed the remainder of the 19 locks into the Summit level—the Summit that divides the waters of the Susquehanna from those of the Schuylkill. Passed Lebanon. Foggy and drizzling; could not see the town. Limestone land; a beautiful country, almost level, the hills low. Buildings are more tasty, some very fine. Bank barns chiefly; many of them thatched with straw. Fence rows clean; very little corn cut up. Before we came to Lebanon we passed through the tunnel. Soon began to descend towards the Schuylkill, down the Tulpehocken from its source. Canal very crooked, winding along the stream. In the evening passed from Lebanon into Berks County. Came 21 miles to-day.

In winter the canals sometimes froze before they could be drained. When this happened they formed a means for recreation (and transportation) for ice skaters in the area. This photo was made on the aqueduct at Newport.

"Manner of living in the boat not very regular. Sometimes we eat breakfast late, mostly one at a time, each one baking his own buckwheat cakes; take 'a piece' for dinner; supper sometimes before night, sometimes after. The locks on the Union Canal, as far as we have come, are built of hewn sandstone, good work, and handsomely coped; better work than in the Pennsylvania locks.

"Friday, Nov. 15.—Started a little before day. Course East, but very serpentine. Country chiefly limestone. Good buildings; some very fine; stone with few exceptions. Stone flouring mills every few miles. Drizzling, and rain in the forenoon, notwithstanding a pleasant day. Came to the Schuylkill a mile or two above Reading. Course East. Stopped for the night opposite Reading; 67 miles from Philadelphia. A break in the Union Canal made it necessary to take the Schuylkill.

"Saturday, Nov. 16.—Started after daylight. Crossed the Schuylkill to the Reading side. Had but an imperfect view of Reading. Saw a number of steeples, a foundry and Keim's nail factory. Saw a locomotive with a train of cars starting for Philadelphia. Three or four miles below Reading crossed the Schuylkill to the South side. The Schuylkill here is not much larger than Pine Creek.

"At three o'clock we passed from Berks into Chester County. Montgomery County on the North side of the river. Distance from Reading, 18 miles. Passed Pottsgrove. It is made up of a few good looking houses. Passed and met a number of Schuylkill boats employed in carrying coal from Pottsville to Philadelphia. Stopped for the night. Four of us lodged in the boat cabin. Upper and nether bunk on each side and very little room in the middle. Rose is stretched on a bed made on a board elevated near the roof. The stove is on one side, the table is at one end, and there is very little room in the middle.

Canal train stalled at Beach Haven (east of Berwick) for lack of water. In a day or two the "break" was repaired and the boats resumed their leisurely journey. Circa 1900. (Courtesy Don Shiner)

"Sunday, Nov. 17.—Started in on another week about daylight. Crossed the river into Montgomery. Good buildings. Some of them fine. Crossed about noon back into Chester County. Stopped opposite Norristown, a handsome little manufacturing town, 16 miles from the city. Boats running thick. Horses, many of them, worried down. Humanity, if no other consideration, should stop the running of boats on the Sabbath; besides a large number of people are deprived of the influence of the Sabbath.

"Staid at Norristown. In the evening went to preaching. Got into the Episcopalian Church, a very fine building, beautifully furnished in the inside with splendid lamps. The minister appeared first in a white gown, then in a black—too much ceremony. Took his text in Acts: 'Those times of ignorance God winked at.' The organ and singers made good music; there were few that sang. Came home to lodge in the boat.

"Norristown is a pretty clever town, 16 miles from Philadelphia, connected with the city by a railroad, besides the one from Reading on the other side of the river. Buildings chiefly rough cast.

"Monday, Nov. 18.—Sold and unloaded the wheat and started empty for Philadelphia, much of the way on the trot."

John Hamilton's account of his return trip home, with boat load of commodities north bound from Philadelphia, is filled with references to ice on the Schuylkill and the Union Canal, which made the going tough.

On one occasion they were frozen in completely, until several hardy boat teams, with more animals on the tow path, broke trail for them.

During the winter freeze the canals were closed for a few months, often completely drained for repairs. Canal boats caught by the final freeze, were simply abandoned till the spring thaw, while the crews rode their mules or horses home for the winter.

One of the most famous, and prolific, writers who traveled the Pennsylvania Canal System was England's Charles Dickens. His impressions of the Portage Railroad appear in that section of this booklet. Read now excerpts from his description of the canal portions of the Main Line, during his trip from Harrisburg to Pittsburgh in 1842:

"It continued to rain heavily at Harrisburg, and when we went down to the Canal Boat (for that was the mode of conveyance by which we were to proceed) after dinner, the weather was as unpromising and obstinately wet as one would desire to see. Nor was the sight of this canal boat, in which we were to spend three or four days, by any means a cheerful one; as it involved some uneasy speculations concerning the disposal of the passengers at night, and opened a wide field of inquiry touching the other domestic arrangements of the establishment which was sufficiently disconcerting.

"However, there it was—a barge with a little house in it, viewed from the outside; and a caravan at a fair, viewed from within; the gentlemen being accommodated as the spectators usually are in one of those locomotive museums of penny wonders; and the ladies being partitioned off by a red curtain, after the manner of the dwarfs and giants in the same establishments, whose private lives are passed in rather close exclusiveness.

"We sat here, looking silently at the row of little tables which extended down both sides of the cabin, and listening to the rain until the arrival of the railway train, for whose final contribution to our stock of passengers our departure was alone deferred. Then a train of three horses was attached to the tow-rope, the boy upon the leader smacked his whip, the rudder creaked and groaned complainingly, and we had begun our journey.

"As it continued to rain most perseveringly, we all remained below; the damp gentlemen round the stove gradually becoming mildewed by

88

Sleeping arrangements on the packet boats, as described by Charles Dickens.

the action of the fire; and the dry gentlemen lying at full length upon the seats, or slumbering uneasily with their faces on the tables. At about six o'clock all the small tables were put together to form one long table, and everybody sat down to tea, coffee, bread, butter, salmon, shad, liver, steak, potatoes, pickles, ham, chops, black puddings, and sausages.

"By the time the meal was over, the rain was nearly over, too; and it became feasible to go on deck; which was a great relief, notwithstanding its being a very small deck, and being rendered still smaller by the luggage. It was somewhat embarrassing at first, to have to duck nimbly every five minutes whenever the man at the helm cried, 'Bridge,' and sometimes, when the cry was 'Low Bridge,' to lie down nearly flat.

"As night came on, and we drew in sight of the first range of hills, which are the outposts of the Allegheny Mountains, the scenery, which had been uninteresting hitherto, became more bold and striking. The wet ground reeked and smoked after the heavy fall of rain; and the croaking of the frogs (whose noise in these parts is almost incredible) sounded as though a million of fairy teams with bells were travelling through the air and keeping pace with us. The night was cloudy yet, but moonlight, too; and when we crossed the Susquehanna River—over which there is an extraordinary wooden bridge with two galleries, one above the other, so that, even there, two boat-teams meeting may pass without confusion—it was wild and grand.

"I have mentioned my having been in some uncertainty and doubt, at first, relative to the sleeping arrangements on board this boat. I remained in the same vague state of mind until ten o'clock or thereabouts, when, going below, I found suspended, on either side of the cabin, three long tiers of hanging bookshelves, designed apparently for volumes of the small octavo size. Looking with greater attention at these contrivances (wondering to find such literary preparations in such a place) I descried on each shelf a sort of microscopic sheet and blanket; then I began dimly to comprehend that the passengers were the library, and that they were to be arranged edgewise on these shelves till morning.

"As to the ladies, they were already abed, behind the red curtain, which was carefully drawn and pinned up in the center; though as every cough, or sneeze, or whisper, behind this curtain, was perfectly audible before it, we had still a lively consciousness of their society.

"My shelf being a bottom one, I finally determined on lying upon the floor, rolling gently in, stopping immediately I touched the mattress, and remaining for the night with that side uppermost, whatever it might be.

"Between five and six o'clock in the morning we got up, and some of us went on deck. The washing accommodations were primitive. There was a tin ladle chained to the deck, with which every gentleman who thought it necessary to cleanse himself (many were superior to this weakness) fished the dirty water out of the canal, and poured it into a tin basin, secured in like manner. There was also a jack-towel. And, hanging up before a little looking-glass in the bar, in the immediate vicinity of the bread and cheese and biscuits, were a public comb and hair-brush.

"At eight o'clock, the shelves being taken down and put away, and the tables joined together, everybody set down to the tea, coffee, bread, butter, salmon, shad, liver, steak, potatoes, pickles, ham, chops, black puddings, and sausages all over again. When everybody had done with everything, the fragments were cleared away, and one of the waiters, appearing in the character of a barber, shaved such of the company as desired to be shaved.

"I may go on to remark that breakfast was perhaps the least desirable meal of the day, as, in addition to the many savory odors arising from the eatables, already mentioned, there were whiffs of gin, whisky, brandy, and rum from the little bar hard by, and a decided seasoning of stale tobacco.

Typical dam and lock arrangement on the Conemaugh River just west of Johnstown. This was lock No. 57 with an 8 foot drop, which opened into the 3-mile pool. This type of canalized river travel was known as "slack-water navigation."

"And yet, despite these oddities—and even they had, for me at least, a humor of their own—there was much in this mode of travelling which I heartily enjoyed at this time, and look back upon with great pleasure. Even the running up, bare-necked, at five o'clock in the morning, from the tainted cabin to the dirty deck; scooping up the icy water, plunging one's head into it, and drawing it out all fresh and glowing with the cold; was a good thing. The fast, brisk walk upon the towing-path between that time and breakfast, when every vein and artery seemed to tingle with health; the exquisite beauty of the opening day, when light came gleaming off from everything; the lazy motion of the boat, when one lay idly on the deck, looking through, rather than at, the deep blue sky; the gliding on at night, so noiselessly, the shining out of the bright stars, undisturbed by noise of wheels or steam, or any other sound than the liquid rippling of the water as the boat went on; all these were pure delights.

"On Monday evening furnace fires and clanking hammers on the banks of the canal warned us that we approached the termination of this part of our journey. After going through another dreamy place—a long aqueduct across the Allegheny River, which was stranger than the bridge at Harrisburg, being a vast, low, wooden chamber full of water—we emerged upon that ugly confusion of backs of buildings and crazy galleries and stairs which always abuts on water, whether it be river, sea, canal, or ditch; and were at Pittsburgh."

# PASSING OF AN ERA

Operation and maintenance of the canals and state railroads was a colossal and expensive proposition for the State of Pennsylvania. The lift locks, (of which there were hundreds), the aqueducts, dams, reservoirs, feeders, canal basins, waste-weirs, tow-path bridges, canal-boat weighing locks, inclined planes, all added to the expense, not to mention the wages of thousands of lock tenders, repairmen, toll-collectors, plane machinery operators, and superintendents. Over the years of operation of canals in Pennsylvania, few actually showed a profit, with the exception of Lehigh Canal and the Monongahela Navigation. Pennsylvania, in the Canal Commissioners report of October 31, 1839, listed a total of 934 miles of state-owned railroads or canals either in operation or being built along the principal rivers of the State. According to McCullough and Leuba's statistics (1976) only 833.61 of state-owned canals were actually completed. The same source also lists 409.70 miles of privately-operated canals within the state borders. By 1855 the state had accumulated a canal debt of 40 million dollars.

At just about the time the Pennsylvania Canals were beginning to pick up the transportation load in this state Robert Stephenson, an Englishman, developed the first really successful steam locomotive, called the "Rocket," which had sufficient power to maintain a speed of 25 to 30 miles an hour and won endurance, pulling, and speed contests sponsored by the Liverpool and Manchester Railway. This event, which occurred in 1829, is generally considered the birth of modern railway travel. There had been railroads previously, but motive power had been horses, or very unsatisfactory steam engines.

Within short order the new steam locomotive was introduced into the United States, as previously mentioned, on the Columbia and Philadelphia Railroad, on the Baltimore and Ohio, which had started construction in 1828, and on the Delaware and Hudson railroad system. Other steam-rail lines followed and within the next ten years America became just as excited about building railroads as they had been about building canals 20 years earlier.

While there were many who felt that canals and railroads could supplement each other, the fact was that the railroads rapidly took away the trade of the tow-path canals after 1852 and eventually replaced them. America's craving for speed diverted its interest in the slow canal boat and put everything on wheels!

The Pennsylvania Main Line's great rival was the Pennsylvania Railroad, chartered in 1846, which began construction of a rail line from

92

End of an era. A rotting canal boat lies abandoned in the canal at Dauphin, circa 1905.

1954. The only stretch of canal that still held water on the Western Division Canal, along the Conemaugh River near Torrance, Westmoreland County.

While excavating for the foundation of the U.S. Steel building, Grant Street, Pittsburgh, 1967, workmen found that the old Grant's Hill Canal Tunnel (lower left) was still there. Upper right is the abandoned "Panhandle Branch" Pennsylvania Railroad Tunnel. (Photo by Myron B. Sharp.)

Exterior of Juniata Aqueduct Number One, looking upstream, circa 1890. An interior photograph is shown on page 25.

Destructive floods terminated the operations of many Pennsylvania canals. However, the Delaware Division, shown here after a flood in 1903, continued operations for another quarter-century. (Courtesy Bucks County Historical Society)

Harrisburg to Pittsburgh the same year. To make rail connections across the state, the railroad first completed its Eastern Division, from Harrisburg to Hollidaysburg in 1850; and then its Western Division, from Pittsburgh to Stone Viaduct, just east of Johnstown, in 1852. By thus making connections with the Portage Railroad as well as the state-owned Columbia and Philadelphia Railroad, (through the independent Harrisburg and Lancaster Railroad) Pennsylvania R. R. in 1852 was able to offer continuous rail service between Philadelphia and Pittsburgh. Brisk passenger and freight traffic began immediately. While the business of the state-owned railroads was unaffected, the Canal Commissioners were shocked at the tremendous reduction in their canal traffic. They rushed through the completion of the North Branch Canal extension, and began building an improved Portage Railroad, without planes, but by February 15, 1854, the date when Pennyslvania Railroad completed its own line over Allegheny Mountain, it was obvious that the Main Line was doomed!

After various Acts and negotiations, the entire Main Line was sold at public auction to Pennsylvania Railroad Company for a mere $7,500,-000—June 25, 1857. On April 21, 1858 a State Act was signed authorizing

95

the Sunbury and Erie Railroad (later acquired by Pennsylvania R. R.) to purchase the Susquehanna Division, the North and West Branch Divisions and the Delaware Division of the State Canal System for $3,500,000. The State had now disposed of all its canals. Hence the Canal Board was formally abolished January 25, 1859.

The Pennsylvania Railroad formed a subsidiary, the Pennsylvania Canal Company, in 1867 which continued to operate various sections of the canal system in the eastern half of the state. The Portage Railroad was abandoned almost immediately, but great improvements were made to the Philadelphia and Columbia Railroad.

The Western Division Canal was abandoned from Blairsville to Johnstown in 1863, and the rest in 1865. The Pennsylvania Canal Company acquired all connecting spurs and extensions of the old Juniata, Susquehanna, and North and West Branch Divisions. They widened and deepened the channel and doubled the length of the locks to permit passage of boats of 260 tons gross load.

Under the new management these canals continued to handle a sizeable volume of freight until about 1875, when business began a steady decline. The great Susquehanna flood of 1889 was a mortal blow to the remaining canals, so that after 1890 all but 144 miles were abandoned. By 1903 the last mile of canal in central Pennsylvania was closed down.

Typical of the sort of thing which was happening on the canals in the late 1800's is the experience of a number of Pennsylvania canal boat captains who returned to the outlet lock on the Susquehanna and Tidewater Canal at Bell's Ferry, Lapidum, Maryland, immediately following a disastrous flood on the Susquehanna in May of 1894.

The flood had caused such damage to the locks, dams and towpath, that the Reading Railroad, operators of the Susquehanna and Tidewater, refused to invest further money in repairs and decided to shut the canal down, for good. Twenty-eight pairs of Pennsylvania Canal boats were caught outside the canal at Lapidum.

The following is the interesting story, as told by Captain Frank Reif, of how he finally brought his boat home:

"On a Saturday night we were towed to Port Deposit, and were landed across the river at Bell's Ferry on Sunday morning. The outlet lock was a single lock and was owned privately by Jacob Tome, a wealthy business man of Port Deposit. Upon landing at this outlet lock we learned that there was a padlock and a chain on the lower gates of the Tidewater Company's double locks nearby and there was no water

Abandoned canal boats at Rupert (near Bloomsburg) after the closing of the canal. Circa 1905. (Courtesy Don Shiner)

in the level. We took the teams out of the boats, made ready to drive them home, and leave the boats to their fate. However, we were told by the other boatmen not to be too hasty. They said there was a stone house a small distance below the locks where tea was sold over the bar at ten cents per drink. It was the custom of the lock tender to loaf at this tea room and the boat men were liberal in buying him drinks. Somehow, that evening the lock tender fell asleep from over imbibing Oolong and when he and the residents of the little town awoke the following morning they were quite surprised at seeing five pairs of boats in the canal, no water in the level and the lock and chain on the gates unbroken. How was it done? That was a mystery thus explained:

"Two men had gone up to the next lock above the foot of Deer Creek, opened the wicket and left sufficient water from the creek to float the boats into the levy after letting five pairs through the locks. When the Reading Company learned that the water was drawn off again and that there were five pairs of boats in the canal they were furious, but thinking it over decided to make repairs to the torn canal to guarantee a 2½' draft, sufficient to float the light boats. This they did. About the time the canal was in readiness for us to pass homeward a man had

One of the last canal boats to pass through the lock at Dauphin on the "Main Line."

made a contract to drag a catch of logs into the canal that had come down the river on the flood and he soon had 8,000 or perhaps 10,000 logs afloat in the shallow ditch. The five boat captains and their crews lost their religion in this predicament, and who would not? There was scarcely water enough to float the boats, and then to have the channel clogged with timber!! We were nine days in progressing eleven miles. To overcome the handicap we put three, sometimes four, teams (16 mules) on one pair of boats in an effort to open the way through the log jam. It was some experience! At times we were obliged to cut the logs apart. Finally we did get through the canal and when the last boats passed the inlet locks we broke the balance beams off the four gates, and that put the big period to the end of the Tidewater Navigation."

Chronologically, some of the other canals throughout the state were shut down in the following sequence: The Swatara Union Canal Feeder closed to navigation in 1862. The Beaver and Erie Canal closed in 1871. The Pennsylvania and Ohio Canal ceased operation in 1872. The North Branch Canal, from Wilkes-Barre to the New York State line, was abandoned in 1872. The Union Canal "gave up the ghost" in 1885. Most of the West Branch Canal, west of Muncy, had shut down by 1891. The Delaware and Hudson ceased operations in 1899. Most of Central Pennsylvania's canals closed down in 1901.

The Schuylkill Navigation shut down gradually between 1872 and 1931, as coal silt deposits extended further and further downstream, filling the navigation channels. The old Delaware Division Canal was turned back to the State, for a park project, in 1931 and 1940.

The Lehigh Coal and Navigation Company reports that the last canal boat captain on the Lehigh Canal was Allen Strohl, of Walnutport, who was hauling coal dirt from Lockport, near Walnutport, to the New Jersey Zinc Company at Palmerton. This operation was terminated by the 1942 flood. Today, there remains in operation in Pennsylvania only the Monongahela River Navigation, now controlled by the U. S. Army Corps of Engineers, which also regulates lockage on the Ohio River.

To the casual reader of history it might appear that the great Pennsylvania Canal and Navigation System of 100 years ago was impractical, financially unsuccessful, and all-in-all a complete failure. However, in spite of the millions of dollars which the State and private operating companies had sunk in the canals, they served a number of important functions. They opened up an avenue of travel to the Ohio River Valley from the East, and to the connecting canal system in Ohio, when no other adequate route existed, at this critical period in the nation's western growth. They gave a tremendous impetus to Pennsylvania's new anthracite coal industry. They developed many of the crossroad settlements throughout the State into sizeable and thriving communities. Even with the heavy tax burden imposed upon them to pay for the canals in the 1840's and 1850s, the people of Pennsylvania prospered greatly as a direct result of the commerce brought to them by the canals.

Appearance of the canal basin at Columbia prior to abandonment, about 1901.

# APPENDIX

In this Appendix we present what we feel is the most extensive collection of data on the Pennsylvania Canals published in modern times. In putting these tables together, we have drawn heavily on the work of those who have gone down this road before — Robert McCullough and Walter Leuba in their excellent "Pennsylvania Main Line Canal" book — Gerald Smeltzer in his "Canals Along the Lower Susquehanna" — Edward M. Kutsch for his fine profiles of the upper and lower Lehigh Canals — the Pennsylvania Department of Forests and Waters for their detailed 1886 map (originally by E.F. Smith, C.E.) of the Schuylkill Navigation — Dr. Ernest Coleman for his detailed research on the Juniata Division and the Bald Eagle and Spring Creek Navigation — Denver Walton for his "Guide to the Beaver Division Canal" — and many others, all of whom are given credit for their contribution at appropriate points, either in the tabular matter, or in the "Acknowledgments" at the rear of this volume.

We have arranged the "Main Line" tables, west to east, from Pittsburgh to Philadelphia, including both canals and railroads; and the publicly operated and privately owned connecting canals in no particular sequence. Much data on the extremities of the Pennsylvania canal system has yet to be retrieved. It is our hope that other dedicated canal buffs will come forth with additional information which can be added to future editions.

Huge, triple-mirrored lanterns, known as "Night-Hawkers", lighted the way at night.

(Taken largely from the report of Sylvester Welch to the Board of Canal Commissioners on November 1, 1830.)

| No. | Lift (ft.) | Type | Location |
|-----|-----------|------|----------|
| 1 | 12.70 | Outlet | Monongahela River, Pittsburgh |
| 2 | 8.93 | Lift | Front and Try streets, Pittsburgh |
| 3 | 8.96 | " | Second and Try streets, Pittsburgh |
| 4 | 8.43 | " | Fourth and Try streets, Pittsburgh |
| 5 | 6 | " | Below Pine Creek, lower Etna |
| 6 | 8 | " | Sharpsburg |
| 7 | 6 | " | Springdale |
| 8 | 6 | " | Lock Street, Tarentum |
| 9 | 6 | " | Mile Lock Lane, Brackenridge |
| 10 | 10 | " | Freeport |
| 11 | | Guard | Leechburg |
| 12 | 10 | Outlet | Apollo |
| 13 | 9 | Lift | |
| 14 | 9 | " | |
| 15 | | Guard | Near Roaring Run |
| 16 | 10 | Guard & Lift | |
| 17 | 10 | Lift | |
| 18 | 9 | " | |
| 19 | 8 | " | |
| 20 | 8 | " | Saltsburg |
| 21 | 8 | " | |
| 22 | 10 | " | |
| 23 | 6 | " | |
| 24 | | Guard | Above Conemaugh tunnel |
| 25 | 10 | Lift | |
| 26 | 10 | " | |
| 27 | 9.25 | " | |
| 28 | 10 | " | |
| 29 | 6 | " | |
| 30 | 0.75 | Guard | Opposite Blairsville |
| 31 | 10 | Outlet | "          " |
| 32 | 8.25 | Lift | "          " |
| 33 | 8 | " | |
| 34 | 10 | " | |
| 35 | 5 | " | |
| 36 | | Guard | |
| 37 | 11 | Lift | |
| 38 | | Guard | |
| 39 | 12 | Outlet | |
| 40 | 8 | Lift | |
| 41 | 8 | " | |
| 42 | 7 | " | |
| 43 | 8 | " | |

Note: This table from
"The Pennsylvania Main Line Canal"
by Robert McCullough and
Walter Leuba

## LOCKS ON UPPER JUNIATA DIVISION
### (Huntingdon Dam to Hollidaysburg)

| Lock No. | Type | Names — Location |
|---|---|---|
| 1 | Outlet | Huntingdon Dam |
| 2 | — | Warrior Bridge |
| 3-4 | Guard & Outlet | Pipers Dam |
| 5-6 | Guard & Outlet | Petersburg Dam |
| 7-8 | — | Above Petersburg |
| 9-10 | — | Near Hatfield's Iron Works |
| 11-12 | — | Alexandria |
| 13 | — | Below Water Street |
| 14 | Outlet | Big Water Street Dam |
| 15-16 | Guard & Outlet | Little Water Street Dam |
| 17-18 | Guard & Outlet | Willow Dam |
| 19-20-21 | — | Below Etna Works |
| 22 | — | "Burnt Lock" Above Etna Works |
| 23-24 | Guard & Outlet | Donelly's Dam |
| 25 | — | "Defords" New Cove Forge |
| 26-27 | Guard & Outlet | Mud Dam |
| 28-29 | — | "Twolocks" — Below Williamsburg |
| 30 | — | "Akes" — Below Williamsburg |
| 31 | — | "Fays" at Williamsburg |
| 32-33 | Guard & Outlet | Williamsburg Dam |
| 34 | — | "Pattersons" — 3-mile Dam |
| 35 | — | "W. Keays" Below Crooked Dam |
| 36 | Guard | at Crooked Dam |
| 37 | — | "Leamers" — Above Crooked Dam |
| 38 | — | "Wises", Below Frankstown |
| 41-42 | Guard & Outlet | at Dam #13 in Frankstown |
| 43-44 | — | "Two Locks" Below Hollidaysburg |
| 45 | — | "Edelman's" Below Hollidaysburg |
| 46 | Guard Lock | at Hollidaysburg |
| — | Weigh Lock | in Hollidaysburg |

## LOCKS ON LOWER JUNIATA DIVISION
### (Duncans Island to Huntingdon Dam)

| Lock No. | Approx. Mileage | Lift or Type | Names — Locations |
|---|---|---|---|
| | 0 | | Duncan's Island Junction Basin (Elevation 362.09') |
| 1 | 0.1 | 8.26' | Just East of Juniata River Aqueduct |
| 2 | 3.1 | — | "Bakers" — Lockford |
| 3 | 7.6 | — | "Roddys" — 2½ miles below Newport |
| 4 | 13.3 | Guard Lock | 91' long — At Millerstown Dam "Slackwater" |
| 5-6 | 13.6 | — | Double-Inlet Lock-Below Millerstown 92'—96' |
| 7 | 19.2 | — | "Thompson's" |
| 8 | 23.3 | — | "Davis" |
| 9 | 27.7 | — | Mexico |

| Lock No. | Approx. Mileage | Lift or Type | Names — Locations |
|---|---|---|---|
| 10 | 30.2 | — | Perryville (above) |
| 11 | 32.7 | — | Mifflin (above) |
| 12 | 33.4 | — | "Rackers" |
| 13 | 36.2 | 5.8' | "Foot of Long Narrows" |
| 14-15 | 41.7 | 7'-5' | "Head of Narrows" |
| 16 | 44.4 | — | Lewistown |
| 17 | — | — | Lewistown (Outlet) |
| 18-19 | 47.2 | 6½'-7' | Granville |
| 20-21-22 | 53.2 | 6'-6.4'-5.9' | Lockport |
| 23 | 59.6 | — | McVeytown |
| 24 | 67.9 | — | "McKinstry's" — Head of 8-mile level |
| 25-26 | 69.6 | Guard-Locks | Aughwick Dam |
| 27-28 | 70.9 | — | "Van Zants", (Upper & Lower Locks) |
| 29-30 | 75.4 | — | 4-locks, "Head of 5-mile Level" |
| 31-32 | 75.8 | — | (Below Mt. Union) |
| 33 | 79.3 | 9' | "Jacks Narrows" ¾ mile below Jackstown Aqueduct |
| 34 | 81.2 | — | "Jamesons" Head of Jacks Narrows |
| 35 | — | — | "Woods" Head of Mill Creek Level |
| 35½ | 85.4 | Guard-Lock | Raystown Dam |
| 36 | 86.1 | — | "Hahns" |
| 37 | 87.4 | — | "Snyders" |
| — | — | Weigh-Lock | Huntingdon |
| 38-39 | 89.7 | — | Lower & Upper Cottage Farm Locks |
| 40 | 91.4 | Guard Lock | Huntingdon Dam |

*(Compiled from data supplied by Dr. Ernest H. Coleman)*

The opening of each new section of canal was the occasion for considerable local celebration. "First boat" is shown here passing through a town on the Juniata Division.

## EASTERN DIVISION LOCKS
### (Columbia Basin to Clarks Ferry Dam)
### Approximate mileage shown

| Lock Name | Approx. Mileage | Lift (ft.) | Other Information |
|---|---|---|---|
| Outlet Lock | 0 | 15.3 | Connection with S & T Canal |
| Columbia Canal Basin | 0 | — | Elevation: 246.58' |
| Chickies | 2 | — | ½ mile north of Chickies Rock |
| Hog Pen | 6 | 19' | Rowena, or Shocks Mill |
| Bainbridge | 11 | — | 1 mile north of Bainbridge |
| Collins | 13 | — | Double Chamber 184' long |
| Scrable | 14 | — | Falmouth — Double |
| Buck Lock | 17 | — | Bucklock Station |
| Neff | 18 | — | 1 mile below Middletown |
| Guard Lock & Outlet Lock | 19 | — | Connection with Union Canal in Middletown |
| Hoyers | 27 | — | Steelton — Double Chamber |
| Harrisburg | 29 | 13.5 | Also a Weigh Lock (1860) |
| Rockville | 34 | 6.88 | Below Rockville R.R. Bridge |
| Dauphin | 37 | 6.99 | Transfer to Northern Central R.R. |
| Twin Tavern | 41 | 6.8 | |
| McKissicks | 43 | — | Guard Lock |
| Clarks Ferry Dam | 43 | — | Slack-Water Pool, Elevation 343.4' |

## PHILADELPHIA AND COLUMBIA RAILROAD
### Names of "Stops" and Mileage from Philadelphia

| Mileage | Station | Mileage | Station |
|---|---|---|---|
| 0 | Philadelphia | 45 | Parkesburg |
| 4 | Hestonville | 48 | Penningtonville |
| 9 | Athensville | 52 | Gap |
| 11 | White Hall | 55 | Kinser's |
| 14 | Morgan Corner | 58 | Lemon Place |
| 17 | Eagle | 63 | Bird-in-Hand |
| 21 | Paoli | 70 | Lancaster |
| 26 | Steam Boat | 71 | Dillerville |
| 30 | Oakland | 73 | Rohrertown |
| 33 | Downington | 78 | Mountville |
| 35 | Gallagherville | 82 | Columbia |
| 41 | Coatesville | | |

*(Listing taken from American Railway Guide 1851,*
*by Curran Dinsmore & Co. N.Y.C.)*

106

One of the many types of horse-drawn rail cars in use on the Columbia and Philadelphia Railroad in the early days of operation.

## LOCKS ON THE SUSQUEHANNA & TIDEWATER CANAL
(Wrightsville, Pa. to Havre de Grace, Md.)

| Lock No. | Mileage | Lift (ft.) | Comments |
|----------|---------|------------|----------|
| Entrance | 0 | — | Wrightsville Dam: Elev. 230.69' |
| 1 | .8 | Guard | Opposite Dam Site |
| 2 | 5.5 | 10.0 | Lower end of "Long Level" |
| 3 | 7.5 | 7.75 | Below Green Branch |
| 4* | 7.8 | 8.46 | Old town of Bridgeville |
| 5* | 9.0 | 7.51 | ¼ mile below Cuffs Run |
| 6* | 10.0 | 8.67 | |
| 7 | 11.5 | 7.6 | ¾ mile below Safe Harbor Dam |
| 8 | 12.0 | 8.45 | ½ mile above Shenk's Ferry |
| — | 14.3 | — | Weigh Lock — York Furnace |
| 9 | 15.6 | 7.25 | Opposite Duncan's Island |
| 10* | 16.0 | 7.85 | |
| 11* | 18.5 | 9.0 | |
| 12 | 19.4 | 8.8 | Located in Lock 12 Park |
| 13 | 19.8 | 8.8 | Slab Tavern |
| 14 | 19.95 | 8.97 | McCalls' Hotel |
| 15 | 21.0 | 8.8 | Hotel |
| 16 | 21.9 | 2.15 | Downstream side of Muddy Creek |
| 17 | 24.0 | 8.70 | |
| — | 25.0 | — | Peach Bottom Village |
| 18* | 26.1 | 10.95 | |
| 19* | 27.5 | 9.7 | |
| — | 27.8 | — | Maryland-Penna. Line |

107

| Lock No. | Mileage | Lift (ft.) | Comments |
|---|---|---|---|
| 1 TWC* | 28.6 | 8.4 | |
| 2 TWC* | 30.0 | 7.7 | |
| 3 TWC* | 31.5 | 9.85 | Old Conowingo |
| 4 TWC* | 32.5 | 9.95 | |
| 5 TWC* | 33.4 | 9.00 | |
| 6 TWC | 34.3 | 9.25 | Just below Conowingo Dam |
| 7 TWC | 36.3 | 11.35 | Opens into Deer Creek |
| — | 37.4 | Guard | Lower end of Dear Creek Slackwater |
| 8 TWC | 38.7 | 10.25 | Also Ft. Deposit outlet Lock |
| 9 TWC | 42.4 | 5.45 | Havre de Grace |

*Locks under water from Safe Harbor, Holtwood & Conwingo Dams

*(Data prepared by W.H. Bosley & E.T. Schuleen*
*of Safe Harber Water Power Corp.)*

## WICONISCO CANAL LOCKS
### (Clarks Ferry to Millersburg)

| Lock No. | Lift (ft.) | Names — Locations |
|---|---|---|
| 1 | 1.85 | Outlet Lock — Clarks Ferry |
| 2 | 8.15 | "Getzes" Upper Lock — Clarks Ferry |
| 3 | 5.99 | "Dittys" Upper Lock |
| 4 | 5.79 | "Dittys" Lower Lock |
| 5 | 5.03 | "Andre's" Lock |
| 6 | 5.38 | Halifax Lock |
| 7 | 9.41 | Guard Lock — Millersburg |

*(Table provided by Dr. Ernest H. Coleman)*

**Picking up a fresh team of horses.**

Fairmount Water Works, Philadelphia, Circa 1830. Wernwag's "Colossus" Bridge across the Schuylkill is shown in the right background. In the foreground is the outlet lock of the Schuylkill Navigation.

## SCHUYLKILL NAVIGATION LOCKS
### (Philadelphia to Port Carbon)

| Lock Name | Approx. Mileage | Elevation Above Lock | Remarks |
|---|---|---|---|
| Fairmount Dam | 0.0 | 10.523 | Outlet to Tidewater |
| Manayunk Canal Outlet | 4.8 | 34.98 | Double Lock |
| Flat Rock Dam | 5.3 | 36.24 | |
| Plymouth Canal Outlet | 9.0 | | Conshohocken |
| Plymouth Dam | 10.0 | 46.01 | Conshohocken |
| Norristown Canal Outlet | 12.3 | | |
| Norristown Dam | 13.8 | 57.50 | Norristown |
| Catfish Dam | 17.5 | 62.33 | Slack-water |
| Pawlings Dam | 20.5 | 66.63 | Slack-water |
| Oaks Canal Outlet | 22.0 | 83.4 | Browers |
| Black Rock Dam | 25.6 | 84.75 | Just above Phoenixville |
| Vincent Canal Outlet | 28.8 | 101.71 | Thro' Royers Ford |
| Vincent Dam | 33.3 | 102.21 | |
| Girard Canal Outlet | 34.3 | 114.27 | Girard Canal Begins |
| Girard Canal Locks (5) | | | |
| Lewis Dam | 57.7 | 178.00 | |
| Poplar Neck Dam | 60.0 | 185.02 | |
| Reading Canal Outlet | 62.0 | | |
| Reading Lock | 64.0 | | Reading Canal |
| Kissinger's Dam | 65.0 | 204.52 | Union Canal Outlet |
| Shepps Dam | 66.0 | 213.23 | below dam |
| Leize's Dam | 67.5 | 221.60 | Slack-water |
| Felix's Dam | 69.6 | 236.41 | Slack-water |
| Duncan's Canal (double) Outlet Lock | 72.2 | | Duncan's Canal Begins |
| Herbine's Dam | 75.3 | 266.09 | |
| Hamburg Outlet Lock | 76.4 | | Leesport |

| Lock Name | Approx. Mileage | Elevation Above Lock | Remarks |
|---|---|---|---|
| Hamburg Canal Locks (4), 3-Double | | | |
| Kernsville Dam | 88.0 | 365.06 | Above Hamburg |
| Blue Mountain Dam | 89.5 | 389.96 | Slack-water |
| Outlet Lock | 91.4 | 400.26 | Port Clinton Canal |
| Hummels Dam | 91.8 | 409.16 | Slack-water |
| Outlet Lock | 92.5 | | ½-mile canal |
| Lord's Dam | 93.0 | 433.11 | |
| Outlet Lock | 94.7 | | Short canal |
| Dam | 95.0 | 444.06 | |
| Outlet Lock | 95.5 | | Short Canal |
| Auburn Dam | 96.0 | 451.36 | Slack-water |
| Tunnel Canal Outlet | 97.3 | | Auburn Tunnel Location |
| Dam | 98.7 | | |
| Outlet Locks (2) | 99.0 | | |
| Dam | 99.3 | | Slack-water |
| Outlet Locks (2) | 99.7 | | Short Canal |
| Dam Lock | 100.3 | | |
| Dam Lock | 100.8 | | |
| Outlet Lock | 101.7 | | Schuylkill Haven |
| Dam | 102.0 | 509.36 | Schuylkill Haven |
| Outlet Lock | 102.4 | | |
| Dam | 102.8 | | Near Cressona |
| — | 104.8 | | Tumbling Run Reservoirs Feeder |
| — | 108.0 | 618.76 | Port Carbon |

*(Many of the Schuylkill Locks are "Staircase" or Double-Locks. Data taken from 1886 map by E.F. Smith C.E., on file in Archives Building, Harrisburg, Pa. Data on section north of Port Clinton incomplete due to early abandonment.)*

A winter scene on Canal Street in Schuylkill Haven, 1883. A Freighter of the type used on the Schuylkill Navigation awaits the spring thaw. (Courtesy Dean Aungst.)

## UPPER LEHIGH CANAL LOCKS
### (Mauch Chunk to White Haven)

| Lock No. | Mileage | Lift (ft.) | Comments |
|---|---|---|---|
| — | 0.0 | — | Mauch Chunk Dam (Elev. 524.6') |
| 1 | 0.607 | 15.3 | Packers Dam #1 Lock |
| — | .694 | | Guard Lock, Upper Kettle Run |
| 2 | 1.491 | 17 | |
| 3 | 2.472 | | Dam #2 Lock |
| 4 | 3.247 | 14 | |
| 5 | 3.475 | 10 | Dam #3 |
| 6 | 3.834 | 21 | |
| 7 | 4.512 | 20 | Dam #4 |
| 8 | 5.392 | 21 | Above Ox Bow |
| 9 | 5.958 | 20 | Dam #5, Little Bear Creek |
| 10 | 7.494 | 16 | Burnt Cabin Flat |
| 11 | 8.028 | 13 | Dam #6 |
| 12 | 8.796 | 21 | Just above Penn Haven |
| 13 | 9.940 | 22 | Dam #7, Potosi |
| 14-15 | 10.456 | 18-20 | Dam #8 |
| 16 | 11.571 | 21 | Dam #9, Stoney Creek |
| 17 | 12.464 | 22 | Dam #10, near Drakes Creek |
| 18 | 13.792 | 25 | Dam #11 |
| 19 | 15.082 | 25.5 | Dam #12, Below Rockport |
| 20 | 16.021 | 25 | Dam #13 |
| 21 | 16.938 | 25 | Dam #14 |
| 22 | 18.019 | 20 | Mud Run |
| 23 | 18.591 | 20 | Dam #15, above M'Minn's Island |
| 24 | 19.497 | 28 | Dam #16, below Hickory Run |
| 25 | 20.976 | 20 | Above Sandy Creek |
| 26 | 21.569 | 25 | Dam #17, below Hay's Creek Run |
| 27 | 23.014 | 30 | Dam #18 |
| 28 | 23.940 | 22 | Dam #19, below Green Mt. Run |
| 29 | 24.849 | 23 | Dam #20, White Haven |
| | | | Head of Slackwater, Elev. 1147.83' |

## LOWER LEHIGH CANAL LOCKS
### (Mauch Chunk Dam to Easton Dam)

| Lock No. | Mileage | Lift (ft.) | Comments |
|---|---|---|---|
| 1 | 0.0 | 1.4 | Mauch Chunk Dam (Elev. 524.6') (Guard Lock) |
| 2 | .51 | 8.3 | Also, Weigh Lock |
| 3 | .76 | 8.3 | Packerton Junction |
| 4 | 1.18 | 9.0 | |
| 5 | 1.60 | 7.2 | |
| 6 | 1.81 | 7.7 | |

| Lock No. | Mileage | Lift (ft.) | Comments |
|---|---|---|---|
| 7 | 2.77 | 9.1 | |
| 8 | 3.48 | 7.9 | Weissport Lock |
| 9 | 3.83 | 8.1 | |
| 10 | 4.27 | 7.8 | |
| 11 | 4.83 | 7.2 | |
| 13 | 5.50 | 12.5 | Parryville Lock |
| 14 | 6.32 | 0.0 | Parryville Dam (Guard Lock) (Elev. 429.3') |
| 15 | 7.04 | 16.2 | Bowman's Lock |
| 16 | 7.89 | 8.2 | Hazzard's Lock |
| 17 | 8.71 | 7.5 | |
| 18 | 9.84 | 7.5 | Just below Palmerton |
| 19 | 10.18 | 4.5 | Aquashicola Aqueduct just above |
| 20 | 10.31 | 9.1 | |
| — | 11.28 | 0.8 | Lehigh Gap Dam (Guard Lock) |
| 21 | 11.91 | 7.9 | |
| 22 | 13.19 | 9.1 | Walnutport Lock |
| 24 | 13.66 | 7.4 | |
| 25 | 14.52 | 5.94 (Est) | |
| 26 | 15.16 | 6.60 (Est) | Just below Bertsch Creek Aqueduct |
| 27 | 15.26 | 7.11 (Est) | Lock Port |
| — | 17.52 | 1.0 | Three-Mile Dam (Guard Lock) |
| 28 | 18.09 | 7.7 | Treichler's Lock |
| 30 | 18.29 | 8.2 | |
| 31 | 20.08 | 9.9 | Slate Dam (Guard Lock) |
| 32 | 20.88 | 7.5 | |
| 33 | 22.21 | 9.5 | Siegfried Lock |
| 34 | 23.46 | 6.4 | Northampton Lock |
| 35 | 23.97 | 7.0 | Just below Hokendaugua Creek Aqueduct |
| — | 24.90 | 0.8 | Swartz's Dam (Guard Lock) (Elev. 274.6') |
| 36 | 25.71 | 7.4 | Catasauqua Lock |
| 37 | 27.00 | 7.4 | |
| 39 | 27.92 | 11.2 | Kimmet's Lock |
| — | 29.21 | 1.4 | Allentown Dam (Guard Lock) (Elev. 247.8) |
| 40 | 29.80 | 7.3 | |
| 41 | 32.73 | 7.2 | Bethlehem |
| 42 | 34.13 | 8.2 | Just below Monocacy Creek Aqueduct |
| 43 | 35.59 | 7.9 | |
| 44 | 37.47 | 8.6 | Freemansburg Lock |
| 45 | 39.44 | 5.7 | Republic Lock |
| 46 | 40.33 | 8.1 | Hope's |
| — | 42.78 | 1.0 | Chain Dam (Guard Lock) Steckel's Lock |
| 47 | 45.06 | 8.6 | Abbott Street Lock, S. Easton |
| 48 | 45.21 | 13.8 | Outlet Lock |
| — | 46.01 | — | Easton Dam (Elev. 169.9') |

*(This data is taken from profiles and tables compiled
by John P. Miller and Edward M. Kutsch in 1978)*

## DELAWARE DIVISION CANAL LOCKS
### (Bristol to Easton)

| Lock No. | Approx. Mileage | Lock Name | Elev. Above Locks | Remarks |
|---|---|---|---|---|
| — | 0.0 | Tidal Lock | 5.5 | Outlet to Delaware River |
| 1-2-3 | 0.3 | | 25.5 | Bristol |
| 4 | 2.6 | Edgely Lock | 31.5 | |
| 5 | 13.3 | Yardley Lock | 37.5 | ½ mile below Yardley Aqueduct |
| 6 | 14.9 | Lear's Lock | 43.5 | |
| 7 | 15.5 | Bordens Lock | 51.5 | |
| 8-9-10-11 | 24.3 | New Hope Locks | 81.3 | Delaware and Raritan Canal Tie-In |
| 12 | 30.6 | Lumberville Lock | 86.6 | Paunaucoussing Creek Aqueduct |
| 13-14 | 32.0 | White's Locks | 101.6 | Pt. Pleasant |
| 15-16 | 34.8 | Smithtown Locks | 113.6 | |
| 17 | 35.8 | Treasure Island Lock | 119.6 | |
| 18 | 39.6 | Uhlertown Lock | 129.6 | Covered Bridge |
| 19 | 41.2 | Lodi Lock | 135.6 | |
| 20 | 46.2 | Narrows Lock | 143.6 | Just below Gallows Run Aqueduct |
| 21 | 48.7 | Durham Lock | 152.6 | Durham Aqueduct |
| 22-23 | 52.5 | Raubsville Locks | 169.9 | |
| 24 | 58.3 | Guard Lock | 169.9 | Easton Dam & Outlet to Morris Canal |

*(Data compiled from a profile by Edward M. Kutsch)*

A well-maintained "level" in the Delaware Division Canal, near New Hope, as it looks today.

# UNION CANAL LOCK DATA

## Lebanon to Reading

| East Locks | Elevation | Mileage |
|---|---|---|
| 1 | 494.5 | 3.59 |
| 2 | 490.0 | 3.59 |
| 3 | 485.5 | 4.42 |
| 4 | 481.0 | 4.86 |
| 5 | 476.2 | 5.01 |
| 6 | 472.0 | 5.37 |
| 7 | 466.5 | 5.98 |
| 8 | 459.5 | 6.36 |
| 9 | 452.5 | 6.37 |
| 10 | 446.5 | 7.26 |
| 11 | 440.5 | 7.61 |
| 12 | 433.5 | 8.16 |
| 13 | 426.5 | 9.00 |
| 14 | 420.5 | 9.45 |
| 15 | 414.5 | 10.05 |
| 16 | 406.5 | 10.44 |
| 17 | 396.5 | 11.34 |
| 18 | 392.5 | 11.88 |
| 19 | 387.5 | 12.37 |
| 20 | 381.5 | 12.63 |
| 21 | 375.5 | 13.24 |
| 22 | 370.5 | 13.78 |
| 23 | 365.5 | 14.18 |
| 24 | 359.5 | 14.91 |
| 25 | 353.5 | 15.79 |
| 26 | 347.5 | 16.45 |
| 27 | 341.0 | 17.51 |
| 28 | 334.5 | 17.71 |
| 29 | 329.5 | 18.24 |
| 30 | 324.5 | 19.46 |
| 31 | 319.5 | 19.96 |
| 32 | 314.5 | 20.65 |
| 33 | 309.5 | 21.50 |
| 34 | 304.5 | 22.14 |
| 35 | 299.5 | 23.51 |
| 36 | 294.5 | 24.39 |
| 37 | 288.5 | 25.74 |
| 38 | 283.5 | 25.89 |
| 39 | 277.5 | 27.00 |
| 40 | 272.5 | 27.89 |
| 41 | 266.5 | 28.56 |
| 42 | 260.5 | 29.99 |
| 43 | 254.5 | 30.93 |
| 44 | 249.5 | 32.00 |
| 45 | 244.5 | 32.86 |
| 46 | 239.5 | 34.29 |
| 47 | 234.5 | 35.21 |

## Lebanon to Reading (Cont'd.)

| East Locks | Elevation | Mileage |
|---|---|---|
| 48 | 229.5 | 36.15 |
| 49 | 224.5 | 36.12 |
| 50 | 219.5 | 37.62 |
| 51 | 211.5 | 38.18 |
| 52 | 206.0 | 39.45 |
| 53 | 198.0 | 40.21 |
| 54 | 188.0 | 41.53 |

## Lebanon to Middletown

| West Locks | Elevation | Mileage |
|---|---|---|
| 1 | 493.6 | 2.30 |
| 2 | 488.2 | 2.49 |
| 3 | 482.8 | 2.69 |
| 4 | 477.4 | 2.86 |
| 5 | 472.0 | 3.15 |
| 6 | 466.6 | 3.40 |
| 7 | 461.2 | 3.54 |
| 8 | 455.8 | 3.71 |
| 9 | 450.4 | 3.87 |
| 10 | 445.0 | 4.00 |
| 11 | 439.6 | 4.14 |
| 12 | 434.2 | 4.31 |
| 13 | 428.8 | 4.49 |
| 14 | 423.4 | 4.70 |
| 15 | 418.0 | 4.81 |
| 16 | 412.6 | 4.94 |
| 17 | 403.6 | 6.04 |
| 18 | 395.6 | 6.12 |
| 19 | 387.6 | 6.28 |
| 20 | 381.6 | 8.13 |
| 21 | 375.6 | 10.63 |
| 22 | 370.6 | 12.69 |
| 23 | 364.6 | 13.40 |
| 24 | 359.1 | 13.54 |
| 25 | 353.6 | 14.78 |
| 26 | 348.1 | 17.34 |
| 27 | 343.1 | 19.32 |
| 28 | 338.1 | 21.67 |
| 29 | 333.1 | 22.96 |
| 30 | 328.1 | 24.82 |
| 31 | 322.1 | 27.96 |
| 32 | 316.1 | 29.12 |
| 33 | 310.1 | 31.11 |
| 34 | 304.1 | 33.77 |

*(The above data was published in "Canals Along the Lower Susquehanna"
by Gerald Smeltzer, 1963)*

## SUSQUEHANNA DIVISION LOCKS
### (Clarks Ferry Dam to Northumberland Basin)

| Lock | Lift (ft.) | Mileage | Remarks |
|---|---|---|---|
| — | — | 0.0 | Clarks Ferry Dam, Elev. 343.4' |
| Outlet | 12.69 | 0.0 | Tip of Duncan's Island |
| Raisiners | 6.0 | 1.0 | |
| — | — | 2.0 | Juniata Junction Basin |
| Buffalo | 7.6 | 5.4 | |
| Montgomery | 7.65 | 8.5 | |
| Mt. Patrick | 6.82 | 10.2 | |
| Lower Liverpool | 6.92 | 12.8 | |
| Upper Liverpool | 6.43 | 14.1 | |
| Dry Saw Mill | 5.4 | 17.1 | |
| Mahantango | 7.65 | 18.9 | Just above Mahantango Creek Aqueduct |
| General Williams | 6.58 | 23.3 | |
| Port Trevorton | 7.63 | 25.3 | Junction with Trevorton Coal & R.R. Co. |
| Shamokin Dam | 1.86 | 36.0 | Guard Lock |
| Outlet Lock | 12.44 | 38.6 | |
| — | — | 38.7 | Northumberland Basin, Elev. 442.4' |

## NORTH BRANCH DIVISION LOCKS
### (Northumberland to Nanticoke)

| Lock | Lift (ft.) | Mileage | Remarks |
|---|---|---|---|
| — | — | 0.0 | Northumberland Basin |
| #1 Lock | 11.49 | 1.2 | Foot of 13-mile level |
| #2 Lock | 11.21 | 14.2 | 2-miles above Danville |
| #3 Rupert's | 10.65 | 21.7 | |
| #4 Bloomsburg | 5.51 | 23.1 | |
| #5 Stoneytown | 9.63 | 30.0 | |
| #6 Berwick | 8.48 | 36.2 | |
| #7 Beach Haven | 8.92 | 39.3 | |
| #8 Guard Lock | 1.93 | 55.8 | Nanticoke "Wide Water Dam", Elev. 514.76' |

*(Note: Basic data taken from the Second Geological Survey of Pennsylvania, 1875-1877)*

Packet Boat "Jennie Bingham" of Freeport ran between Pittsburgh and Blairsville. (Model by I. M. Jones, Carnegie Museum.)

## WEST BRANCH DIVISION LOCKS
### (Northumberland to Lock Haven)

| Lock | Lift (ft.) | Mileage | Remarks |
|------|-----------|---------|---------|
| — | — | 0.0 | Northumberland Canal Basin, Elev. 442.4' |
| #13 | 7.75 | 0.6 | |
| #14 | 5.94 | 6.5 | |
| #15 | Outlet | 8.0 | Cross-cut Connection to Lewisburg |
| #16 | Guard Lock | 8.2 | Past Lewisburg Dam |
| #17 | 6.12 | 10.2 | Milton Lock |
| #18 | 5.2 | 14.6 | Watsontown |
| #19 | 7.2 | 22.0 | Montgomery |
| #20 | 5.4 | 22.9 | Muncy Dam Lock |
| #21 | 5.5 | 24.0 | |
| #22 | 5.5 | 26.2 | Muncy |
| — | — | 27.5 | "Muncy Cut," ¾ mile |
| #23 | 6.5 | 28.8 | Wash Taylor's Locks |
| #24 | 5.07 | 29.0 | Near Hall's Station |
| #25 | 6.12 | 33.2 | Joe Philips Lock |
| #26 | 4.83 | 35.4 | Head of "White Water" |
| — | — | 35.9 | Loyalsock Creek Dam |
| #27 | 6.3 | 36.2 | Montoursville Lock |
| — | Outlet | 39.5 | Outlet to River at Williamsport |
| #28 | — | 41.2 | Located East of Lycoming Creek Aqueduct |
| #29 | — | 50.2 | Near Thomas Smith Tract |
| #30 | — | 51.7 | "Wild Man's Lock" |
| #31 | — | 53.9 | Larry's Creek Lock & Aqueduct |
| #32 | — | 56.4 | Jersey Shore Lock |
| #33 | Guard Lock | 66.4 | Below Bald Eagle Dam |
| #34 | — | 68.4 | Lock Port Lock |
| — | — | 73.4 | (Terminus at Farrandsville) |

(A slack-water connection via Bald Eagle Dam was made with the Bald Eagle & Spring Creek Navigation across the river, at Lock Haven.)

116

Passenger-carrying Packet Boat "Pittsburgh". 72′ long, 11′ feet wide and 8′ high. Inside was ladies' cabin, gentlemen's cabin and cook-room. Capable of handling 150 passengers. (Carnegie Museum model.)

## BALD EAGLE & SPRING CREEK NAVIGATION LOCKS
### (Bellefonte to Lock Haven)

| Lock | Lift (ft.) | Approx. Mileage | Remarks |
|------|-----------|-----------------|---------|
| — | — | 0.0 | Bellefonte Dock |
| #1 | 7.0 | 0.3 | |
| #2 | 10.0 | 0.5 | |
| #3 | 9.0 | 0.8 | |
| #4 | 5.0 | 1.6 | |
| #5 | 8.5 | 1.9 | Milesburg |
| #6,7,8 | 10.0(each) | 3.5 | |
| #9 | 8.5 | 4.1 | |
| #10 | — | 4.8 | Guard Lock |
| #11 | 8.0 | 5.3 | |
| #12 | 7.3 | 5.7 | |
| #13 | — | 6.3 | Guard Lock |
| #14 | 8.5 | 6.6 | |
| #15 | 7.0 | 7.3 | |
| #16 | — | 7.6 | Guard Lock |
| #17 | 8.75 | 8.6 | |
| #18 | 9.5 | 10.3 | Howardville |
| #19 | 7.75 | 11.3 | (Howard Furnace) |
| #20 | — | 11.7 | Guard Lock |
| #21 | 7.75 | 12.6 | |
| #22 | 9.0 | 14.0 | |
| #23 | — | 14.5 | Guard Lock |
| #24 | 9.5 | 15.9 | |
| #25 | — | 16.9 | Guard Lock |
| #26 | 9.5 | 18.9 | |
| #27 | 6.0 | 20.5 | |
| #28 | 6.5 | 21.0 | |
| — | — | 25.1 | Lock Haven, Outlet to Slackwater Dam & |

Total Lockage 183¼ feet.   Lock-Port on North Side of Susquehanna.

*(Note: This data taken from 1835 Map by M.R. Stealey, Engineer, supplied by Dr. Ernest H. Coleman. Mileage includes the "Bald Eagle Cut.")*

117

# DELAWARE AND HUDSON CANAL LOCKS
## (Lackawaxen to Honesdale)

| Lock No. | Lift (ft.) | Comments |
|---|---|---|
| #1,2,3 | — | Eliminated By Roebling Aqueducts |
| #4,5,6 | 8-10-10 | Ridgeway Locks |
| #7 | — | Tinsmith's (Joe Tague) |
| #8 | — | O'Donnells |
| #9 | — | Bishops (Gulf Island) |
| #10 | — | George Rowland's |
| #11 | — | Saxon's (Larson's) |
| #12 | — | Westfalls |
| #13-14 | — | Griswold's Locks |
| #15 | — | Jim Avery's (Blooming Grove Island) |
| #16 | — | Corkonian's |
| #17 | — | Rodger's |
| #18 | — | Jim Hanner's |
| #19 | — | Abe Rowland's (Van Aken's Island) |
| #20 | — | Pat Gannon's |
| #21 | — | Field Bend (Opposite Feeder Dam) |
| #22-23 | 11-10 | Harrison's Locks |
| #24 | — | Frank Danniel's (Punch Camp Island) |
| #25 | 10 | Pulpit Basin |
| #26 | — | Baisenville |
| #27 | — | Carroll's (Billy O'Brien) |
| #28 | — | Rock Lock (Mike Connors) |
| #29 | 10 | Lower Hawley (Conklin's) |
| #30 | 10 | Weigh-Lock Basin, Hawley |
| — | — | Hawley Basin and Pa. Coal Co. Gravity RR Terminal |
| #31 | — | Wier's (O'Han's) |
| #32 | — | McKahill's |
| #33 | — | White Mills |
| #34 | — | Lonesome Lock |
| #35 | — | Tom Whitaker's |
| #36 | — | Chris Alen's Boat Works |
| — | — | Guard Lock, Honesdale |
| #37 | 11 | Entrance to Canal Basin and D. & R. Gravity RR Terminal |

*(Data taken from "Coal Boats to Tidewater" by Manville B. Wakefield, 1965)*

# GUIDE TO THE BEAVER DIVISION CANAL
## *By Denver L. Walton*

0.0 Mouth of the Beaver River. Beaver Point on the east bank, Stone's Point on west. Joins Ohio River at Mile 25.5.

0.3 Girard Locks, No. 16 and 17 (named for Stephen Girard, Philadelphia philanthropist). Oversized locks (25' x 120') permitted passage of steamboats to pool above Dam No. 6. Bridgewater, on the west bank, was the main canal terminus. Freight was transferred here to steamboats, or canal boats passed through locks and were towed on the Ohio River to Pittsburgh. The west abutment of the Dam remains. Lock No. 17 covered by Ohio River pool raised in 1936 by Montgomery Island Dam. Lock No. 16 serves as a foundation for the Rochester sewage pumping station. The river wall is visible. Canal to slackwater pool (No. 5.)

2.4 Blount Lock, No. 15. This, and all remaining locks on the Beaver Division were 15' x 90'. This is the first of a flight of four locks and a one mile stretch of canal. Lock No. 15 can be seen from the Fallston Bridge. It is partly covered, but the curved lower end of the river wall is visible.

2.5 Boyle's Lock, No. 14. Covered by the Railroad embankment.

2.6 Buck Woods' or "Butt Cut," Lock No. 13. Covered by the railroad embankment.

2.7 Van Lear's Lock, No. 12. Covered by the railroad embankment. No trace of former canal bed above this point exists.

3.8 Dutchman's Lock, No. 11, and Dam No. 5. The river wall of the lock is visible. The dam was built in 1826 for water power and was incorporated into the canal system in 1831, then rebuilt in 1869, with a 20 foot fall. Across the river, part of the Beaver Falls water power canal remains. Some freight was moved on this waterway by boats which crossed the slackwater pool above the Dam (No. 5). In 1976, two local industries (Mayer China and Republic Steel) were using the canal for hydro-electric power. Canal to slackwater pool (No. 4).

4.8 Canal resumed separate channel. Drill marks in native stone on shore show location.

4.9 Bannon's Lock, No. 10. Ten foot lift. Nothing remains.

5.1 Farrow's Lock No. 9. The west wall of this lock is tumbled and scattered, but easily recognized. The right wall is covered by the railroad embankment. Five foot lift.

5.3 Dam No. 4, built 1832. (The first dam on the Beaver River was built there prior to 1800.) The slackwater pool (No. 3) above the dam was called the "Seven Mile Level." Entry channel remains.

12.3 Mouth of the Connoquenessing Creek. Canal crossed on slackwater. This is the site of the incident in which young James Garfield nearly drowned.

12.4 Rock Point Lock, No. 8 and Dam No. 3 (8 foot lift). A short stretch of watered canal remains, but there is no trace of the lock or dam. Metheney's Tavern, built in 1836, offered shelter to travellers on the canal and later the New Brighton and New Castle Railroad. Building collapsed in 1936, the foundation remains. Canal to slackwater (No. 2).

*Mile*

14.0 The improved river channel in this stretch was called "Hard-scrabble" because the current was swifter here than in other parts of the canal, and upstream travel was relatively more difficult.

16.6 Beaver Division Lock, No. 7 (10' Lift). Locksite remains, some stone in place, but badly ravaged by flood waters over the years. Site of the former village of Staylesville, now completely gone. Short stretch of canal on either side of the lock.

16.7 Dam No. 2. No trace visible. Canal to slackwater (No. 1).

18.6 Beaver Division Lock, No. 6 (9 foot lift), and end of slackwater navigation on the Beaver River. No trace of the lock, which was located below East Moravia at the point where the river swings to the west.

18.9 Beaver Division Lock, No. 5 (9 foot lift). Located along Canal Street in East Moravia, about 100 yards north of Penna. Route 168. Locksite discernible by topography. A dry dock was located just above this lock. A well preserved stretch of towpath extends from here to Lock No. 4.

19.2 Beaver Division Lock, No. 4 (9 foot lift). Discernible by topography. A few stones remain. Best remaining section of towpath at this point.

19.8 Northernmost visible trace of the Beaver Division Canal—the wet ditch between the highway and railroad at the underpass opposite the Penn Power generating plant.

21.7 New Castle Junction. The Pennsylvania and Ohio Canal joined the Beaver Division Canal at this point. The P&O led to Youngstown, Warren, and the Ohio and Erie Canal at Akron. The canal crossed the Shenango River on an aqueduct, then followed the Mahoning River west to Ohio. There are no visible remains of the canal in Pennsylvania.

22.5 Beaver Division Lock, No. 3 (9 foot lift). Covered by railroad tracks, and no trace remains. Site is 0.7 miles north of railroad crossing, near Mahoningstown bridge.

22.3 Beaver Division Lock, No. 2 (10 foot lift). Covered by railroad tracks, and no trace remains. Site is just south of Gardner Avenue, adjacent to Big Run.

23.4 Big Run Aqueduct Foundation of existing railroad trestle across Big Run may be part of the aqueduct base.

24.3 Beaver Division Lock, No. 1. Near former Rosena Furnace. Covered by single railroad track east of Croton Avenue.

24.4 Dam on Neshannock Creek (not numbered). No trace remains. Canal crossed on slackwater above dam, between existing Grove Street and Mill Street bridges. Spur canal extended southwest along Neshannock Creek to the iron industries below.

24.7 Beaver Division crossed New Castle on route adjacent to South Street, then entered the Shenango River above Dam No. 1, of which no trace remains. Canal to slackwater pool.

29.0 Western Reserve Harbor, terminal port on the Beaver Division.

31.0 Nominal end of the Beaver Division Canal, based on mileage stated in engineering reports. The Erie Extension began here and led to Sharon, Greenville, Meadville (via the French Creek Feeder), and Erie. The Extension was completed in 1845.

## PENNSYLVANIA CANALS: PRIVATELY BUILT

(All mileage shown is within the state)

| Canal | Miles |
|---|---|
| Delaware & Hudson, | |
|     Honesdale, Pa. to Rondout, N. Y. | 25.00 |
| Schuylkill Navigation, | |
|     Port Carbon to Philadelphia | 108.23 |
| Lehigh Coal & Navigation, | |
|     White Haven to Easton | 71.75 |
| Union, | |
|     Reading to Middletown | 77.64 |
| Pine Grove Feeder, | |
|     Union Canal to Pine Grove | 22.00 |
| Conewago, | |
|     Around Falls of Susquehanna River | 1.25 |
| Susquehanna & Tidewater, | |
|     Columbia, Pa. to Havre de Grace, Md. | 30.00 |
| Pennsylvania & Ohio, | |
|     New Castle, Pa. to Akron, Ohio | 18.00 |
| Beaver & Sandy, | |
|     Glasgow, Pa. to Bolivar, Ohio | .75 |
| Junction, | |
|     Athens, Pa. to Elmira, N. Y. | 3.25 |
| Conestoga Navigation, | |
|     Lancaster to Susquehanna River | 18.00 |
| Codorus Navigation, | |
|     York to Susquehanna River | 11.00 |
| Muncy Cut, | |
|     Muncy to West Branch of Susquehanna | .75 |
| Spring Creek and Bald Eagle Navigation | |
|     Bellefonte to Bald Eagle Cut | 22.08 |
| Total | 409.70 |

| Canal | Miles |
|---|---:|
| Main Line: | |
| Eastern Division, | |
| Columbia to Clarks Ferry | 42.85 |
| Juniata Division, | |
| Juniata Aqueduct to Hollidaysburg | 127.32 |
| Western Division, | |
| Johnstown to Pittsburgh | 104.25 |
| Allegheny Outlet, | |
| Western Division to Allegheny River | .75 |
| Kittanning Feeder, | |
| Kittanning to Western Division | 14.00 |
| Susquehanna: | |
| Susquehanna Division, | |
| Clarks Ferry to Northumberland | 41.00 |
| North Branch Division, | |
| Northumberland to New York State Line | 169.00 |
| West Branch Division, | |
| Northumberland to Farrandsville | 73.00 |
| Bald Eagle Cut, | |
| Lock Haven and Bald Eagle Creek | 4.00 |
| Lewisburg Cut, | |
| West Branch Division to Lewisburg | .75 |
| Wiconisco Line, | |
| Clarks Ferry to Millersburg | 12.25 |
| Beaver and Erie: | |
| Beaver Division, | |
| Ohio River at Beaver to Pulaski | 30.75 |
| Shenango Division, | |
| Pulaski to Conneaut Lake | 61.00 |
| Conneaut Division, | |
| Conneaut Lake to Erie | 45.50 |
| French Creek Feeder, | |
| Bemus' Mill to Conneaut Lake | 25.00 |
| Franklin Line, | |
| French Creek Feeder to Franklin | 22.44 |
| Delaware: | |
| Delaware Division, | |
| Easton to Bristol | 59.75 |
| Total | 833.61 |

*(Both tables from "Pennsylvania Main Line Canal",
by McCullough and Leuba.)*

122

## LIST OF STRUCTURES ON MAIN LINE PENNSYLVANIA CANAL.

| DIVISION. | EXTENT OF DIVISION. | Length of Divisions in Miles. | Miles Feeder. | Miles Slack Water. | Miles Canal. | Lockage Feet. | Outlet Locks. | Guard Locks. | Lift Locks. | Weigh Locks. | Total Locks. | Road Bridges. | River Bridges. | Farm Bridges. | Towing Path and Winding Bridges. | Foot Bridges. | Total Bridges. | Number of Aqueducts. | Total Length of Aqueducts. | Number of Dams. | Total length of Dams. | Number of Culverts. | Waste Ways. |
|---|---|---|---|---|---|---|---|---|---|---|---|---|---|---|---|---|---|---|---|---|---|---|---|
| Eastern Division............ | From Columbia to Susquehanna Junction, | 46 | ... | 27 | 45.7 | ... | 4 | 2 | 23 | 1 | 30 | 38 | 1 | 42 | 11 | 9 | 101 | 11 | ... | 2 | 2241 ft. | 16 | 10 |
| Lower Juniata Division............ | From Susquehanna Junction to Head of Guard Lock, Huntingdon Dam, | 90 | ... | .16 | 89.8 | ... | 2 | 3 | 33 | 1 | 39 | 42 | ... | 37 | 7 | 8 | 89 | 18 | ... | 5 | 2887 | 46 | 27 |
| Upper Juniata Division............ | From Head of Guard Lock, Huntingdon Dam, to Hollidaysburg | 87 | ... | 16.5 | 20.5 | ... | 18 | 13 | 20 | 1 | 47 | 18 | ... | 19 | 29 | ... | 66 | 5 | ... | 14 | 3322 | 2 | 17 |
| Totals East. and Jun. Division | | 178 | ... | 17.0 | 166.0 | ... | 19 | 18 | 76 | 3 | 116 | 98 | 1 | 98 | 47 | 12 | 256 | 34 | ... | 21 | 8400 | 64 | 54 |
| Lower Western Division............ | From Lower Outlet Lock at Pittsburgh to head Guard Lock, Blairsville Dam, inclusive, | 73 | ... | 18. | 55. | ... | 5 | 6 | 20 | 1 | 32 | 52 | ... | 43 | 18 | 7 | 120 | 10 | ... | 5 | 2340 | 22 | 24 |
| Upper Western Division............ | From head Guard Lock, Blairsville, to Johnstown, | 80 | ... | 9. | 21. | ... | 5 | 6 | 25 | 1 | 36 | 16 | ... | 11 | 10 | 1 | 87 | 5 | ... | 7 | 2047 | 12 | 14 |
| Total Western Division......... | ............ | 103 | ... | 27. | 76. | ... | 10 | 11 | 46 | 2 | 68 | 67 | ... | 54 | 28 | 8 | 157 | 16 | ... | 12 | 4387 | 34 | 38 |
| Total East. and Jun. Divisions. | ............ | 173 | ... | 17. | 166. | ... | 19 | 18 | 76 | 3 | 116 | 98 | 1 | 98 | 47 | 12 | 256 | 34 | ... | 21 | 8400 | 64 | 54 |
| Total on Canal ...... | | 276 | ... | 44. | 232. | ... | 29 | 29 | 121 | 5 | 184 | 165 | 1 | 152 | 75 | 20 | 413 | 49 | ... | 33 | 12787 | 98 | 92 |

Length given for Dams does not include embankment at Reservoirs.

We are indebted to Dr. Ernest H. Coleman and Charles Mann of State College, Pa. for their intensive research work in locating this table of information, compiled by the Pennsylvania Railroad Company in 1859, shortly after their purchase of the "Main Line" from the State of Pennsylvania. It was found in the 13th Annual Report of PRR, in the Rare Book Room of Pattee Library. Some variations will be noted in this table from other data in this book, due to alternate designations for the junction of the Eastern and Susquehanna Canal Divisions.

# THE AUTHOR

The family of William H. Shank, professional engineer, historian and lecturer, has been associated with the Pennsylvania canal system through five generations. Michael F. Shank, an immigrant German ship's carpenter, settled in Liverpool, Pennsylvania in 1820, and built some of the first canal boats to operate on the Susquehanna Division Canal. Michael's son, John Shank, operated a canal travelers' hotel at Liverpool. Wilson Webster Shank, son of John, was an employee of the Pennsylvania Railroad at Williamsport when that company was still operating many sections of the canals. Clyde Updegraff Shank, son of Wilson, as a young engineer ran surveys along the Bald Eagle and Spring Creek Canal. William Shank, son of Clyde, is currently concerned with canal history. He was instrumental in forming the Pennsylvania Canal Society as Secretary and Vice President and is currently President of the American Canal Society, formed in 1972. He has lectured on canal history in all corners of Pennsylvania and neighboring states. He has also authored and published the following historical works: "Vanderbilt's Folly," "Historic Bridges of Pennsylvania," "Indian Trails to Superhighways," "Great Floods of Pennsylvania," "History of the York Pullman Automobile," "York — First Capitol of the United States, 1777-1778," and "Three Hundred Years with the Pennsylvania Traveler."

The Author, with a copy of one of his recent books — THREE HUNDRED YEARS WITH THE PENNSYLVANIA TRAVELER. The author's son, J. William Shank, whose photo appears on the mantle, was the prime illustrator of this book.

# THE ILLUSTRATOR

PHILIP J. HOFFMANN, P.E.
Engineer — Historian — Artist
1891-1973

The late Philip J. Hoffmann of Johnstown, Pennsylvania, was born in Albany, N.Y., February 22, 1891. Phil early made his mark as an artist. His brother-in-law, Karl V. Eckel, holds a 1909 newspaper photo captioned "Philip Hoffmann, whose clever drawings are on exhibition at the Albany High School." For this, Phil was awarded a gold medal. After graduation from Rensselaer Polytechnic Institute, he came to Johnstown in 1913, as an engineering employee of Cambria Steel Company, now a division of Bethlehem Steel. During World War I, with the Motor Transport Corps, Unit 302, in France, Phil spent his spare time making drawings which his friend Dr. Ernest Coleman, describes as "pencil sketches of historic and architecturally magnificent structures that are elegant in terms of beauty, detail and shading, together with a portrayal of depth that is all but three dimensional."

A registered professional engineer, Phil Hoffmann also engineered the Little Conemaugh River "cut off" through the ridge which was pierced by the old Allegheny Portage Railroad tunnel, and designed a 50″ diameter water main, running from South Fork to the present Bethlehem Steel plant, much of it along the old Portage Railroad route. As a result of this activity he acquired a considerable interest in the Portage Railroad and its connecting canal systems in Johnstown and Hollidaysburg. This has lead to the hundreds of detailed sketches which he made after retirement, in pencil, pen and color, of "life as it was" on the Pennsylvania canal system of the mid 1800's. His attention to historic detail in these sketches is known only to those of us who have had the great pleasure of working with him to assure their correctness.

W.H.S.

# ACKNOWLEDGEMENTS

I wish to express my deep appreciation for the support of the following individuals in the preparation of this book and its predecessors. Some of them have graciously spent much time in researching data, sketches, photos and even text material of their own — to make this book more comprehensive. All of them have lent me their moral support in my canal historical endeavors:

Paul B. Beers, Harrisburg
Dr. Ernest H. Coleman, State College
Col. Robert E. Felsburg, P.E., Harrisburg
Earl B. Giles, Johnstown
Capt. Thomas F. Hahn, Ed.D., Shepherdstown, (W.Va.)
Col. Russell E. Horn, P.E., York
Edward M. Kutsch, Douglassville
Walter Leuba, Pittsburgh
Robert S. Mayo, P.E., Lancaster
John P. Miller, Bethlehem
Richard Steinmetz, Camp Hill
Dr. George F. Swetnam, Glenshaw
Denver L. Walton, Monaca
George R. Wills, Lebanon                                    W.H.S.

# REFERENCES

"The Pennsylvania Main Line Canal"—Robert McCullough & Walter Leuba (1976)
"Pennsylvania Transportation"—George Swetnam (1968)
"Canals Along the Lower Susquehanna"—Gerald Smeltzer (1973)
"The Switzerland of America"—Theo. L. Mumford (1886)
"Past and Present"—Blair County Historical Society (Spring-Summer, 1964)
"The Pennsylvania Canals"—Historic Pennsylvania Leaflet No. 1—Hubertis Cummings (1957)
"The Columbian"—Columbia County Historical Society (Oct. 1960)
"The Canals of Pennsylvania"—Theodore B. Klein (1901)
"Lancaster County Historical Society—Papers"—Volume XXXIX—No. 3 (1935)
"The Historical Journal"—Vol. 1, No. 4, Williamsport, Pa. (August 1887)
"Pa. Canal, Indiana & Westmoreland Counties"—Clarence D. Stephenson (1961)
"Pa. Board of Canal Commissioners' Records"—Hubertis M. Cummings (1959)
"Monongahela River Navigation Charts"—U.S. Army Engr. Dist. Pittsburgh (1965)
"Centennial History, Pennsylvania Railroad Co."—George H. Burgess & Miles C. Kennedy (1949)
"Guide to the Historical Markers of Pennsylvania"—Pennsylvania Historical & Museum Commission (1957)
"Old Towpaths"—Alvin F. Harlow (1926)
"Allegheny Portage Railroad"—Pa. Railroad Information Vol. 2, No. 1 (Feb. 1930)
"The Portable Boats of Early Railroad Practice"—J. Snowden Bell (1920)
"Notes on Samuel Martin Kier"—W.K. Cadman (1961)
Report of Sylvester Welch, Engineer, Portage Railroad (Nov. 1, 1833) (As published in The Historical Journal, Williamsport, July 1887)
"The Schuylkill Navigation"—Edwin F. Smith, Philadelphia (1905)
"Josiah White, Prince of Pioneers"—Eleanor Morton (1946)
"Coal Boats to Tidewater"—Manville B. Wakefield (1971)
"Canals & Railroads of the Mid-Atlantic States 1800-1860"—Hagley Foundation (1981)

# OTHER PUBLICATIONS OF THE AMERICAN
# CANAL AND TRANSPORTATION CENTER

JOURNEY THROUGH PENNSYLVANIA—1835, Edited by William Shank (1981). Reprint of a book published by Philip Nicklin of Philadelphia in 1836, describing in detail a trip he made across Pennsylvania by canal, rail and stage coach. His alliterative original title was "A Pleasant Peregrination Through the Prettiest Parts of Pennsylvania Performed by Peregrine Prolix". Illustrated with Hoffmann and Storm sketches, as well as old photographs.

THE COLUMBIA-PHILADELPHIA RAILROAD AND ITS SUCCESSOR—William Hasell Wilson, 1896. This book is an on-the-spot account of the building of one of the oldest railroads in America by its chief engineer, later resident engineer for the Pennsylvania Railroad, who purchased it from the Pennsylvania Canal Commissioners. This 1985 reprint is fully illustrated with 45 old photos, maps and drawings from the files of William H. Shank.

THE CANALLER'S SONG BOOK—By William Hullfish, Music Instructor, Writer, Singer (1984). This 88 page, 8½ x 11 book contains forty historic canal ballads (words and music) collected from old records in the northeastern USA over a ten year research period. Illustrated with old canal drawings.

HISTORY OF THE YORK-PULLMAN AUTOMOBILE, 1903-1917—By William H. Shank, (1970). History of the "Six-Wheeler" Pullman, and its successors, which almost made York, Pa. the automotive capital of the United States. History of the early automotive industry in Eastern Pennsylvania also included. Profusely illustrated. An ideal gift for antique car buffs.

TOWPATHS TO TUGBOATS—A History of American Canal Engineering. By Shank, Mayo, Hahn and Hobbs (1985). The works of such famous Canal Engineers as Benjamin Wright, Canvass White, Charles Ellet, William Hamilton Merritt, George Washington Goethals are detailed — with the canals they built. The Erie, the Welland, the "Soo", the Panama, the St. Lawrence Seaway and the Tenn-Tom are among the many waterways described in detail. A 72-page, 8½ x 11 book, the publication contains more than 130 drawings, maps and photographs in USA, Canada and overseas.

ELLET AND ROEBLING—By Donald Sayenga, (1983). The story of the interplay of the lives of these two famous canal and bridge-builders of the 1800's and their magnificent suspension structures, some of which still stand today. Fully illustrated.

WHEN HORSES PULLED BOATS—By Alvin F. Harlow. A 1983 reprint of Harlow's little-known canal book, written for school students in 1936. An excellent exposition of the historic canal era in the USA. Introduction by William H. Shank. Canal bibliography included. Illustrations by Orson Lowell and Philip Hoffmann.

TOWPATH GUIDE TO THE CHESAPEAKE AND OHIO CANAL—By Thomas F. Hahn, (1985). A fully illustrated, historical commentary and mile-by-mile directory for the entire 184-mile length of the C. & O. Canal Towpath from Washington, D.C. to Cumberland, Maryland. Excellent maps included.

HISTORIC BRIDGES OF PENNSYLVANIA—By William H. Shank, (1986 Edition). Traces the development of the bridge-building arts from the time of the first covered bridge in America, built in Philadelphia in 1805, to modern bridges of the 20th Century. Biographies of such famous bridge builders as John Roebling, Theodore Burr, Charles Ellet and Ralph Modjeski included. Profusely illustrated.

CHESAPEAKE AND OHIO CANAL OLD PICTURE ALBUM—By Thomas F. Hahn (1985). One hundred excellent full-page photographs from the 1800's show peak operations along the C. & O. Canal, from Georgetown to Cumberland, Maryland. The introduction includes a brief history of the canal and much additional historical information appears in the photo captions.

GREAT FLOODS OF PENNSYLVANIA—A TWO-HUNDRED YEAR HISTORY— W. H. Shank, (Fifth Printing, 1981). Data, photos and non-technical text on all major floods in the Keystone State since records have been kept. A definitive work.

SYLVESTER WELCH'S REPORT ON THE ALLEGHENY PORTAGE RAILROAD, 1833—Detailed description, by its chief engineer, of one of the most unusual railroads ever built in the United States. A series of ten, steam-powered, inclined planes were part of this amazing railroad. Illustrated with Hoffmann drawings. Fold-out map included, (Fourth printing, 1983.)

THE C & O CANAL — AN ILLUSTRATED HISTORY—By Thomas F. Hahn & Diana Suttenfield-Abshire (1981). A full-size, illustrated sketch book of historic scenes and engineering features along the entire 184-mile length of the C & O Canal. 84 pages of excellent sketches and explanatory captions.

VANDERBILT'S FOLLY — A HISTORY OF THE PENNSYLVANIA TURNPIKE— W. H. Shank, (Eighth Printing, 1985). The railroad war of 1880-85 which created the tunnels and roadbed for the present turnpike. History of the Turnpike, 1940-1985, included.

INDIAN TRAILS TO SUPERHIGHWAYS—By William H. Shank, (1982 Printing.) History of the development of Pennsylvania's historic roads and the many interesting vehicles used on them. Much Indian folklore and early colonial history. Descriptions of Braddock's Road, Forbes' Road, National Highway, Lancaster Turnpike, Plank Roads, Corduroy Roads, William Penn Highway, Lincoln Highway, Pennsylvania Turnpike and Keystone Shortway. Profusely illustrated.

THE C. & O. CANAL BOATMEN, 1892-1924—By Thomas F. Hahn (1980). The Life and Times of the men who worked the canal boats in the declining years of the canal's operation. Prepared after careful study of tapes and written interviews with boatmen, many of whom have since passed on. The book abounds with direct quotations from many of them.

THE BEST FROM AMERICAN CANALS—A three-volume series by members of the American Canal Society, published over a 14-year period (All 8½ x 11, 88 pages each and profusely illustrated):
PART NUMBER I—(1972-79) Features the canals of Northeast USA, the Deep South, Illinois & Wisconsin, Canada, Ireland, England, Egypt, and Europe.
PART NUMBER II—(1980-83) History and travel along the Canals of New York State, Ohio, Pennsylvania, New Jersey, Maryland, Virginia and Indiana; New England, Florida, the Panama Canal, the Trent-Severn, the Rideau, and Canals of Germany and Thailand.
PART NUMBER III—(1983-86) Canals of New England, metropolitan New York area, Erie Canal, American Waterways, Lehigh & Schuylkill Canals, Virginia Canal Tunnels, the I & M Heritage Corridor, the Tenn-Tom, the St. Lawrence Seaway, Panama Canal, English Canal Cruises, Canals of Sweden, Germany and India.

Inquiries may be directed to the American Canal and Transportation Center, 809 Rathton Road, York, Pa. 17403. Price list and discount schedule available.